THE CLASSICS SLACKER READS
THE SCARLET LETTER

Copyright © 2021 by Cta Negrón
ISBN: 9798517525918
[Set in Minion]
Illustrations by Kris Wraight
Designed by tslapointedesign.com
"Slacky" drawing by Eliza B.
Text by Deb Martin, Heidi Mastrogiovanni,
and Cta Negrón

The Classics Slacker gratefully acknowledges the
inspiration of those two crazy kids and "friends"
Herman Melville and Nathaniel Hawthorne, who turned
white and red into enduring literary colors.

"*O foolish and tiresome little brook! Why art thou so sad? Pluck up a spirit, and do not be all the time sighing and murmuring!*"—PEARL

CONTENTS

INTRODUCTION

Hello there, Slackies! Nice to see you again! So what have you been doing since reading *The Classics Slacker Reads Moby Dick* and *The Classics Slacker Reads Madame Bovary?* Waiting breathlessly for the next installment of the series, right? Well, lucky you, because here it is: *The Classics Slacker Reads The Scarlet Letter.*

The Classics Slacker is not gonna lie to you (The Classics Slacker will never lie to you, unless it's in service to the God of Comedy); this one was a wee bit of a slog.

Published by American author Nathaniel Hawthorne in 1850, *The Scarlet Letter* was one of the first mass-produced books in America. It was an immediate bestseller and has inspired numerous stage, television, and film adaptations. (Demi Moore and Gary Oldman starred as the illicit lovers in the 1995 version, for example, and can you say "steamy"?) British novelist D. H. Lawrence called *The Scarlet Letter* a "perfect work of the American imagination."

Umm…okay…granted, it is likely without peer when the American imagination turns specifically to thoughts of adultery and condemnation in a Puritan New England colony during the seventeenth century.

And, yes, Hawthorne was writing from the perspective of having been born in Salem, Massachusetts (that jolly town of the fabled witch trials), when the nineteenth century was young, but, wow, every kind of reader of modern sensibilities will find something puzzling, if not downright disturbing, in *The Scarlet Letter.*

Twenty-first century feminists will wince at the unequal consequences meted out by the powers-that-were for extramarital hanky-panky. "Bingo!" if you guessed that the woman in this tale bears the brunt of society's condemnation, what a surprise.

Modern proponents of the separation of church and state will consider it no excuse that the story unfolds well over a century before that most profound principle of our United States was enshrined in our Constitution, because my *god*, does religion ever play a role in Hester Prynne's tragic fate.

And today's indulgent helicopter parents will be alternately shocked by the harshness of the way Puritan society includes an innocent child in its judgment and scandalized by how often the kid is left to go on her merry way completely unsupervised. Also, she has to do her own homework.

Yes, it's a challenging journey Hawthorne offers his readers of the future. Nonetheless, please join The Classics Slacker to witness a few dreary years with Hester and her husband and her boyfriend and her daughter and a big, ol' honkin' letter in neon red (not really neon as that gas probably wasn't yet harnessed for ornamental use by mankind) and a whole buncha stern-faced (is there any other kind?) Puritans. Because if the great D. H. Lawrence thought this novel was flawless, who is The Classics Slacker to say otherwise?

1

INTRODUCTORY TO THE SCARLET LETTER (HAWTHORNE IS A BIG FAT LIAR)

*In which there's already a lot that
The Classics Slacker is finding hard to swallow*

Many classic books begin with momentous lines that often become as iconic as the book itself: "It was the best of times. It was the worst of times." "It is a truth universally acknowledged, that a single man in possession of a good fortune, must be in want of a wife." And perhaps the most famous of all, the immortal, the indelible, the unforgettable: "Call me Moby."

Then there is *The Scarlet Letter* by Nathaniel Hawthorne. Our man Nate does not use the catchy first sentence technique favored by his BFF Herman Melville. Nor does he put his main characters into action (with a capital A) right from the get-go. No. Hawthorne opens his most celebrated work (celebrated by whom we're not sure—it's a very grim book) with an introduction of some 15,000 words that has nothing to do with the plot of the novel.

That any reader endured sentences such as "It is now nearly two centuries and a quarter since the original Briton, the earliest emigrant of my name, made his appearance in the wild and forest-bordered settlement, which has since become a city. And here his descendants have been born and died, and have mingled their earth substance with the soil; until no small portion of it must necessarily be akin to the mortal frame wherewith, for a little while, I walk the streets" while slogging his or her way onward toward the main story testifies to the tragically meager diversions in the greater Boston area in 1850. Heck, they couldn't even opt for reading lighter fare like *Moby Dick*; it wouldn't be published for another year.

Hawthorne scholars generally agree that the only reason their favorite author wrote such an overblown introduction was to increase the length of his novel. It was already finished when he went back and added the introduction. His publisher must have said, *A book? You call this a book? Why, it's no thicker than a paper napkin. Now go make it longer before I use it to wipe my butt!* Lacking modern word processing tools, Hawthorne couldn't boost the page count by widening the margins to the size of submarine sandwiches. He had no choice but to write more words, mind-numbing piles of 'em. Words like perforce, prolix, and prate.

Most of the introduction chronicles his deathly dull days working as a Custom-House officer and the even more deathly dull men he worked with. Toiling there cut into his writing time, like, a wicked lot. But there were many eminent personages for Hawthorne to observe and many names to drop, such as Emerson, Longfellow, and Alcott (dad of Louisa May). He even went skinny dipping with Thoreau. Now *that* tidbit woke up The

Classics Slacker for thirty seconds to almost a minute.

The introduction should've ended there because how could it become more titillating than that? But Hawthorne reports an even more exciting fact: Chaucer was also a Custom-House officer. Great. But The Classics Slacker would like to point out that Chaucer didn't prattle on at the beginning of *The Canterbury Tales* with a "Hey, I'm a Custom-House officer and let me tell you all about it. When you get to the end of my belaboring the subject nearly to asphyxiation, and only then, can you read 'The Pardoner's Tale.' "

In short, irony intended, "The Introductory" is one big who cares. While trudging through this material, The Classics Slacker was justifiably hating on Hawthorne. The Classics Slacker, like all human beings, has limited time on this earth and Hawthorne was robbing The Classics Slacker of precious life minutes. They were spinning down the drain like that lady's blood in the shower scene in *Psycho*.

More pages, more pages, more pages and then—lightbulb! Hawthorne has an idea to vaguely connect the introduction of *The Scarlet Letter* with the rest of the book, also called *The Scarlet Letter*. With only a few pages left in the introduction, he slaps down a big ol' lie. He says that one day, while he was snooping around the second floor of the Custom-House, he found an old piece of *scarlet* cloth in the shape of a capital letter A!

And also, get this, Hawthorne then finds "several foolscap* sheets" about a woman named Hester Prynne who really existed!

Wow, wicked cool, so the book you're about to read—no, just kidding, you're not, because The Classics Slacker has already done that for you—is based on a true story! Omigod. Except, it's not!

The Classics Slacker did some research, and there is no evidence that the whole "I found a big, red A and also Hester Prynne really existed and I have the documents to prove it" is even true!

Shame on you, Nate, you big fat liar!

It's a good thing Shakespeare wasn't a Custom-House officer like Hawthorne. You would open up a copy of *Hamlet* and instead of enjoying a super spooky scene of a foggy castle and a ghost, you'd be forced to read the author's introduction first, which would begin: "Hey, I'm Bill Shakespeare and I'm a Custom-House officer and write plays on the side. The other day after work I just happened to be walking through a cemetery and picked up a skull that was lying on the ground. I'm not sure why, but I decided to start talking to it. Anyway, here's Act I, scene i."

* "Foolscap" is just an old-timey word for paper. Why is it called foolscap? The Classics Slacker neither knows nor cares, having been bored into a near coma well before Hawthorne dropped foolscap into his agonizingly incomprehensible introduction.

2
THE ROSE KNOWS

In which a rose bush beautifies a cheerless opening scene

As if he were tuckered out from writing an introduction that runs the length of the Massachusetts Turnpike, Hawthorne manages an opening chapter of only 487 words. And those words are grim. There are no scenes of famous writers frolicking naked in pristine lakes or even the bustling hum of the Custom-House.

Now we are set squarely in Puritan New England, which is so not a place you would want to live, trust The Classics Slacker on this. A bunch of people are standing in front of a locked door, as if they are waiting for the supermarket to open on Senior Citizens Wednesday. It's a forlorn-looking group: "A throng of bearded men, in sad-colored garments and gray, steeple-crowned hats, intermixed with women, some wearing hoods and others bareheaded…"

Upon closer inspection, it becomes clear that the building they are congregated in front of is not a Safeway, it's a prison:

THE CLASSICS SLACKER READS THE SCARLET LETTER

"A wooden edifice, the door of which was heavily timbered with oak, and studded with iron spikes." Yikes! Iron spikes! A maximum-security prison, no less. So why is everyone standing there? They can't all be waiting to post bail for their brother who got busted for selling weed.

We're not going to find out. Not in this little chaplet anyway. Instead, we learn more about the prison—it's not only ugly, gloomy, dark, and rusty, it's overgrown with "unsightly vegetation."

So this is how *The Scarlet Letter* begins: dour people crowding around a dreary prison door. Why even read on? Well, Hawthorne does attempt to end the chapter in a more positive vein by referencing a wild rose bush that stands right by the threshold of the prison. He hopes it will "symbolize some sweet moral blossom that may be found along the track, or relieve the darkening close of a tale of human frailty and sorrow."

Seriously, stick around and hang in there with me, Hawthorne seems to be saying when he offers a bloom to his audience: "We [Hawthorne is using the royal we here] could hardly do otherwise than to pluck one of its flowers, and present it to the reader." The reader could accept it with pleasure.

On the other hand, that same flower could prick the reader's finger causing blood to spurt or trigger a bout of uncontrollable sneezing if the reader is allergic to roses. In which case the reader will head to the bathroom for bandages and/or tissues and will never reach the next chapter.

Which might not be the worst thing.

3
GIVE ME AN A!

*In which Hester Prynne's scarlet letter makes
its much-anticipated debut*

The same bunch of people from the preceding chapter are still standing around the prison door as if they're waiting for *Hamilton* tickets. Hawthorne gives a sense of how over-the-top merciless the crowd is by describing them as "stern-browed men" and "unkindly visaged women." If anyone else were wearing the expressions plastered on these townspeople's faces, it would have to be in anticipation of something really awful happening, say a hanging or a whipping or a flash mob shaking it to "Sussudio" by Phil Collins.

Hawthorne further observes that the women in the group are especially chubby (they have "broad shoulders and well-developed busts"). He theorizes that their looks come from being not too many generations removed from Queen Elizabeth I and calls the Virgin Queen "man-like." Who knew that fat-shaming in this country had such early origins?

When the first of these frowning matrons says something, we finally learn who they are expecting to emerge from the prison. She says that "malefactresses as this Hester Prynne" would not be getting off nearly so easy if the women had chosen her punishment rather than the "worshipful magistrates," who are all wussy men. Indeed, one matron suggests branding Hester on the forehead and a second, "the ugliest" and "most pitiless" of them all, says Mistress Prynne should have been sentenced to death for her sin.

If, as Madeleine Albright once said, there's a special place in hell for women who don't support other women, then these gals are riding the express train straight to Hades, that's for sure. The A train, one assumes.

Another sturdy woman adds that "the Reverend Master Dimmesdale, her godly pastor, takes it very grievously to heart that such a scandal should have come upon his congregation."

This is some major foreshadowing. The Classics Slacker can't tell you why just yet because that would fall right into the "spoiler alert" category, so you'll just need to trust The Classics Slacker on this.

At last the big moment arrives. The aforesneered Ms. Prynne emerges from the prison. At first, she is led by the "town-beadle" who tries to show Hester he's in charge. But she snaps him a major Z (that's right, not an A), and wordlessly conveys that he is most emphatically not the boss of her: "…he laid his right [hand] upon the shoulder of a young woman, whom he thus drew forward; until, on the threshold of the prison-door, she repelled him, by an action marked with natural dignity and force of character, and stepped into the open air as if by her own free-will."

Go, Hester! Shake it off!

She's wearing a fabulous dress with a red A embroidered on

the front in gold thread. The letter is an important element of the story. We know this because Hawthorne keeps capitalizing SCARLET LETTER. One wonders if he is going to shout it like that for the entire book, which would be extremely annoying.

Oh, and just in case any readers needed another reason to loathe this cruel community, Hester is carrying a three-month-old baby, who "winked and turned aside its little face from the too vivid light of day; because its existence, heretofore, had brought it acquaintance only with the grey twilight of a dungeon, or other darksome apartment of the prison."

Are you getting this? The infant hadn't seen the sun before because it had spent the entirety of its new life in a freakin' prison. Clearly, when the Baby Jesus this crowd admires so much was handing out compassion, they were all, like, No thanks, I'm good.

At first Hester holds the baby close to hide her SCARLET LETTER. But then she's, like, *What the heck am I hiding? So I had sex. So what? And my embroidery handiwork is awesome. It should be shown off.* She practically tosses the kid aside to reveal every stitch on the SCARLET LETTER.

There's more. Instead of withering away in prison, as the crowd had surely expected, Hester actually looks even better than when she went into the slammer. *And* she's even transformed that badge of shame into the new fashion must-have with her stitching: "...the point which drew all eyes, and, as it were, transfigured the wearer—so that both men and women who had been familiarly acquainted with Hester Prynne were now impressed as if they beheld her for the first time—was that SCARLET LETTER, so fantastically embroidered and illuminated upon her bosom."

No question, our girl looks fine. Her SCARLET LETTER, Hawthorne tells us, "was so artistically done, and with so much fertility and gorgeous luxuriance of fancy, that it...was of a splendor in accordance with the taste of the age." She has taken what the dour townsfolk intended to be her punishment and turned it into some grade-A bling. Which may have been a misstep, given her neighbors' no-fun natures and the fact that Hawthorne tells us that her fancy A was "greatly beyond what was allowed by the sumptuary regulations of the colony."

Yep. She's a feisty tart who is ignoring the sumptuary regulations. That is not going to inspire those "hard-featured" goodwives to clasp her to their well-developed busts or make her reentry into this cheerless Puritan society any smoother. Just sayin'.

The beadle (come on, it even *sounds* like an insect) yells for a path to open so Hester can be led to the scaffold. (Hawthorne writes "sort of scaffold," which makes one wonder how it is like or unlike a scaffold and why would anyone care.) She climbs up the platform to finish out her sentence of standing there for three hours.

Just standing. And holding her baby. Clearly the lack of childcare in the prison system is a long-standing problem. Long-standing. Get it?

Oh la-dee-da. Ho-hum. This is boring. Hester's mind fills up the hours by going back in time and watching her life pass before her eyes. There is her dad in his Elizabethan ruff and her mom telling her not to run across the street. There are "sports" (did she play lacrosse?). There's a memory of an uneven-shouldered old guy. (Who might he be? Stay tuned. More about him later.)

The bubble bursts, the wavy lines straighten, and Hester pops back into reality where she just can't believe that she's standing on a sort of scaffold, carrying a baby, and wearing a SCARLET LETTER. She actually touches it to confirm. Yep, still there.

4
STAGE FRIGHT

In which the past comes galloping into town
on a horse with no name

Hester is still standing on the scaffold and the people are still standing watching her stand. If only there were a karaoke machine nearby both for her and their entertainment, the situation would be much improved. Things become even worse when she sees a man in the crowd with seriously uneven shoulders. This upsets her so much she squeezes her baby too hard, and the baby cries, and you know this can't be good.

Crooked-shoulder man's reaction to seeing Hester isn't much better: "A writhing horror twisted itself across his features, like a snake gliding swiftly over them..." Well, ew.

Clearly something has gone down between these two. So the crooked-shoulder man turns to the nearest level-shouldered townsman and says, Hey, Pal, I'm new in these parts. I was "long held in bonds among the heathen-folk to the southward." (Isn't that interesting?) What's up with this gal and the scaffold 'n' stuff? Well, the townsman is all, like, Pal, you do *not* wanna know, and the man with the wonky shoulders is all, like, Yeah, I do, so the guy tells him: Hester Prynne was "left to her own misguidance" when her husband sent her ahead to Massachusetts while he stayed back in England to do some stuff. That was two years ago so you know that baby isn't her husband's, and then the stranger tells him, "Ah!—aha!—I conceive you," and The Classics Slacker wanted to smack the stranger for making that stupid pun.

The townsman also tells the crooked-shouldered stranger, Aren't you glad you showed up in our swell town where we punish our ladies just right? Feel free to join us as we stand here watching her stand. Oh, and we're just itching to hear her name the father of her baby, too.

The townsman then goes on to tout the caring qualities of the "Massachusetts magistracy" because they could have given naughty Hester the death penalty, but instead, "in their great mercy and tenderness of heart they have doomed Mistress Prynne to stand only a space of three hours on the platform of the pillory, and then and thereafter, for the remainder of her natural life to wear a mark of shame upon her bosom."

Wow, y'all are swell! Such humanity! Such compassion! Has anyone nominated y'all for the Nobel Peace Prize yet?

The stranger then surprised The Classics Slacker by saying, "It irks me, nevertheless, that the partner of her iniquity should not at least, stand on the scaffold by her side. But he will be known—he will be known!—he will be known!"

Wait, *what?* Is this guy a feminist? A seventeenth-century advocate for women's rights and equal treatment under the law? Wow, wouldn't that be a twist!

Also note that chanting "will be known" three times is basically the Puritan equivalent of Dorothy clicking the heels of her ruby slippers together and intoning "There's no place like home."

At this point a big ol' booming voice from above calls out Hester's name in a "loud and solemn tone."

"HESTER PRYNNE…"

God?

No. It's just a bunch of magistrates, Governor Bellingham, et. al., on the balcony overlooking the scaffold. Because who doesn't love an open-air get-together to watch a public shaming? When Hester looks up at them, she realizes that the crowd before her was dripping with compassion compared to this grim gang. These dudes, members of local government and the clergy, want her to dish the name of the baby's father, presumably so the mystery impregnator can also be punished. The Classics Slacker supposes they are just looking for one more person to slap a letter on, Puritans being very judgmental that way. If this keeps up, the whole town is going to look like a huge bowl of alphabet soup.

Anyway, one of these balcony bros, Reverend Wilson, commands Hester to spill the tea, and she drops a big ol' nope-bomb on that order. So Governor Bellingham hands the inquisition reins over to a wan young minister by the name of Reverend Arthur Dimmesdale. Dimmesdale is seriously pale. Hawthorne describes him as pale at least four times within two pages. He should have named him Dimmespale.

Beyond describing his skin tone, Hawthorne also tells the reader that Dimmesdale "had come from one of the great English universities" and that "so far as his duties would permit, he trod in the shadowy by-paths, and thus kept himself simple and childlike, coming forth, when occasion was, with a freshness, and fragrance, and dewy purity of thought, which, as many people said, affected them like the speech of an angel."

So, let's see if The Classics Slacker has this right: He smells good, he's smart, and he's kind of a baby man? Okay, whatevs.

The fragrant (and pale, did we mention pale?) Reverend Dimmesdale tells Hester, "I charge thee to speak out the name of thy fellow-sinner and fellow-sufferer! Be not silent from any mistaken pity and tenderness for him; for, believe me, Hester, though he were to step down from a high place, and stand there beside thee, on thy pedestal of shame, yet better were it so than to hide a guilty heart through life."

Ohh, Reverend, how you *do* talk!

But Hester's lips stay zipped (or perhaps buttoned, since the zipper was not yet invented) and Reverend Dimmesdale is thinking, *Whew, that was a close one.* SPOILER ALERT: The Classics Slacker might as well tell you right now that Reverend Dimmesdale is the one who worshipped at Hester's prynne, if you catch The Classics Slacker's drift. Hawthorne holds off revealing this information for several chapters, but The Classics Slacker is under no such obligation.

Hester has already suffered plenty on the scaffold, but it's about to get worse as Reverend Wilson begins to gas on about sin. He will continue to do so for the better part of an hour. And you know that whole time Hester is thinking, *Rev. Wills? If I tell you the name of the guy who knocked me up, will you put a sock in it already? Sheesh!*

5
LET'S TALK OVER DRINKS

In which the crooked-shouldered stranger pours cocktails for Hester and her baby

Just for fun, let's make a list of places throughout the ages we'd all rather be than in prison in Puritan New England, shall we?

1. Hauling those massive building blocks to construct the Pyramids of Giza
2. Shoeless at Valley Forge with Washington's troops in the dead of winter
3. Wearing a fancy wig and headpiece in Paris during The Great Terror
4. In the "Order Here" line at Chick-fil-A

The vagaries of time and place notwithstanding (you know a combo meal at any fast-food joint would sound pretty good to our heroine right about now), Hester Prynne clearly agrees that she is stuck in one of the worst locations in history. When she is brought back to her cell, she is "like a possessed one" and her poor baby "writhed in convulsions of pain."

Fortunately for Hester, the warden ushers in a man of medicine. Unfortunately for Hester, he's that guy with the mismatched shoulders from the crowd scene. Hester freezes when she sees him, and he asks the warden to leave him alone with her, and oh my god, what's going to happen now?

The stranger's name "was announced as Roger Chillingworth"—because Hawthorne loves nothing more than whacking his readers over the head with glaring messages in the monikers he chooses for his characters. Chillingworth says he learned about natural medicine when he was being held hostage by savages (which really does sound like a euphemism, doesn't it?) and mixes a potion to help the baby. He tells Hester, You give it to her because it's not like she's *my* baby or anything.

And Hester hesitates because she's afraid that this guy might be trying to poison her baby. Then Mr. I'm-Not-a-Doctor-but-I-Play-One-in-Prison turns all snippy. "Foolish woman! What should ail me to harm this misbegotten and miserable babe?"

Good point. But Hester still can't bring herself to do it, so he grabs the kid and gives her the medicine, and, thank goodness, she is soothed and falls asleep. Chillingworth then turns his medical attention to Hester.

He takes her pulse, makes her say "ahh," raps her knee with that little reflex hammer, and thinks it over. Yep, got it. I know just the drink for you. Hester's certainly hoping it's a vodka tonic. But even if he did break out the Tito's, she'd still be apprehensive about downing any kind of drink concocted by this super creepy guy. But what the heck, the baby is doing fine so…down the hatch!

After all the doctoring is over, the two fall into a conversation wherein they call each other "thee" and "ye" and "thou" a lot. And they speak in incomprehensible sentences, using words such as "behoof" and "wottest" and "wast." The Classics Slacker spent undue hours trying to deciphereth their meaning based on context and finally broke through. Here's an example of a modern sentence using those words: "Yo, Greg, thou wottest get a beer? I wast at a great microbrewery yesterday and I behoof a tasty IPA."

But Hester and Chillingworth (brrr… it's a metaphor, get it?) don't talk beverages. No. Because now, Ladies and Gentlemen, it is time for a Big Reveal! This stranger, as it turns out, is Hester's husband, aka not the father of her child because remember that part about them not seeing each other for two years and remember that stuff about the gestation period for humans being nine months?

He basically says the situation was all his fault (good of him) because he married her when he was already "decaying" (just how old is this guy anyway?) and she was blooming. And he stupidly thought that his being a scholar would be enough to captivate her. Hester puts the brakes on that right away and good for her for speaking up! "[T]hou knowest that I was frank with thee. I felt no love, nor feigned any." (And then there was the aforementioned absence of two years.)

Chillingworth concedes the point and when Hester laments, "I have greatly wronged thee," he actually responds with a bit of the grace that has been little in evidence anywhere in town, saying that they have wronged each other. (Perhaps a foreshadowing of no-fault divorce laws.) But, hey, while we're on the subject, what's the name of that schmuck who wronged us both?

Oh, noo, Hester responds, nice try to catch me off guard, but *no way* will I ever tell you his name, like, never.

Chillingworth assures her that he will not be giving up in his quest to find out who the guy is anytime soon, like, *never*. "He bears no letter of infamy wrought into his garment, as thou dost, but I shall read it on his heart. Let him live! Let him hide himself in outward honor, if he may! Not the less he shall be mine!"

Ohh, boy. Remember that guy Ahab and his endless pursuit of the white whale? (Please refer to the flagship book in this series, *The Classics Slacker Reads Moby Dick*.) He's starting to look super easygoing compared to the faux physician Chillingworth.

Chillingworth makes Hester swear that she will not divulge his identity (great, another secret) to anyone by threatening to get really pissed at the guy who got her pregnant if she does. Hester agrees right away because she doesn't want to see her more-or-less ex-husband do anything crazy. Hester, girrrl, The Classics Slacker is right there with you in wanting no part of that.

6
STICKING IT TO THE TOWNSPEOPLE

In which Hester receives some reparations
by selling her fancy fashions

Hester is free now, having served three months in prison and three hours on the scaffold. She could live anywhere. Given the circumstances, you would think she would catch the next type of whatever method of travel was fastest at that bygone time—The Classics Slacker wasn't in a Googling mood, so let's just go with...maybe horse? Instead, Hester chooses to remain in the area. She finds a charming little one-bedroom with a thatched roof just outside of town within walking distance to a beach.

Perhaps Hester decides to stay in Tsk-Tsk Town because there's no place like home, even though home is a place where everyone is mean and judgmental. There are a few other reasons, too, which Hawthorne is all too happy to expound upon.

"Her sin, her ignominy, were the roots which she had struck into the soil. It was as if a new birth, with stronger assimilations

21

than the first, had converted the forest-land, still so uncongenial to every other pilgrim and wanderer, into Hester Prynne's wild and dreary, but life-long home."

No, seriously, huh? She's not leaving why?

Hawthorne also says that Hester wanted to remain in the place where the unnamed father of her baby resides and also some stuff about Hester hoping that her daily shame would purge her soul, or some blather like that. But The Classics Slacker had stopped listening by then. In case thou hast not noticed, our man Nathaniel has a bad habit of tossing in a wealth, a plethora, an abundance of words. His comparatively slim tale is padded like a bronco buster's bum after a long weekend at the rodeo.

So Hester lives this lonely little existence in her cottage by the sea. But she has one thing going for her. She is a talented seamstress and needlework artist. Her pieces are highly sought after.

"Deep ruffs, painfully wrought bands, and gorgeously embroidered gloves, were all deemed necessary to the official state of men assuming the reins of power…the array of funerals… baby-linen…there was a frequent and characteristic demand for such labour as Hester Prynne could supply." Yeah, Hester? We *love* that fancy needlework of yours, but we sure don't like *you,* and we're certainly not inviting you to any of our events, public or private. So will my lace petticoat be done by Tuesday?

Hawthorne points out that despite all the demand for regalia for ceremonies and baptisms and funerals, Hester was never "called in to embroider the white veil which was to cover the pure blushes of a bride."

No, because, seriously, those townsfolk may be rank hypocrites, but that doesn't mean they don't have values! Can't be too careful; wouldn't want to leave any adultery stains on your virginal blushing brides.

In her spare time, of which she probably had none because, you know, it's not like there were a lot of time-saving conveniences available (and also, she's a single mom), Hester makes lovely clothes for her baby and sews garments to give to the poor. Are the poor appreciative? No, they are not. They, too, leap on the Let's All Punish Hester Train.

There is very little respite from the contempt Hester endures, which is to say, none. She can't even enjoy peace and serenity within the walls of her church. If she went inside, "it was often her mishap to find herself the text of the discourse."

Our thanks to the choir for that beautiful hymn. The subject of today's homily will be a crowd favorite and the one you all enjoyed last week and the week before and also for the entire month of June; namely, that red-letter-wearing slut who lives down by the water...

Seriously, even kids are nasty to Hester, which should come as no surprise, because you know the kind of dreck they're hearing at home:

"...they pursued her at a distance with shrill cries, and the utterances of a word that had no distinct purport to their own minds, but was none the less terrible to her, as proceeding from lips that babbled it unconsciously."

Hawthorne leaves it to the reader to guess what terrible name the kids are calling her. The Classics Slacker is going to take a shot in the dark here and go with "Adulterer." Although it could also be "Alien," "Anchovy," or "Attorney."

The whole situation is so stressful, poor Hester starts to lose it a little, and imagines she can intuit the sinful and immoral stirrings of the people around her. Talk about a useless superpower:

"Sometimes the red infamy upon her breast would give a sympathetic throb, as she passed near a venerable minister or magistrate. 'What evil thing is at hand?' would Hester say to herself. Lifting her reluctant eyes, there would be nothing human within the scope of view, save the form of this earthly saint!"

"Earthly saint," our earthly tuchus! But dear Hester, it seems, just can't be as cynical or clear-sighted as The Classics Slacker is. "Hester Prynne yet struggled to believe that no fellow-mortal was guilty like herself."

Hester, they *are* guilty, okay? Take The Classics Slacker's word for it; those Prissy Pedantic Puritans have a lot of nerve being such Pious Prejudiced Pills. You know, let he who is without sin cast the first stone and all that other stuff about forgiveness in the Bible that they seem to have conveniently forgotten.

Do *not* get The Classics Slacker started…

7

PEARL:

A DIFFERENT KIND OF GIRL

*In which the reader is reminded that in nature
a pearl is created via lots of irritation*

Most authors deftly and seamlessly introduce new characters into an ongoing story. Not our Hawthorne, he of the "Hey! I found a red piece of fabric in the shape of an A on the floor of the Custom-House." When he discovers that a few chapters have gone by without any mention of Hester's daughter, he opens the next chapter with "We have as yet hardly spoken of the infant..." No, not "we," Nate, "you." Or thou. Or thee. The Classics Slacker respects whatever pronoun you choose for yourself but refuses to let you implicate The Classics Slacker in this misogynistic nightmare.

Yay! thinks Pearl—named for being her "mother's only treasure"—I get my own chapter!

Of course she does. Hawthorne doesn't vilify Hester's baby.

In fact, he points out that God forgives where Man judges. "God, as a direct consequence of the sin which man thus punished, had given her a lovely child." So there, you miserable, miscreant meanies. God is on Hester's side.

Still Hester isn't getting it. She's totally bought into the "I did an evil deed" deal, so every minute she's sweating it out with Pearl, expecting her daughter to sprout neck plugs, hair snakes, psoriasis. "Day after day she looked fearfully into the child's expanding nature, ever dreading to detect some dark and wild peculiarity that should correspond with the guiltiness to which she owed her being."

Hawthorne doesn't help out much by referring to Pearl as a little elf, an airy sprite, a miniature demon.

And truth be told, despite her diminutive size, Pearl is kind of a handful. She throws rocks and stuff at other kids. She zings flowers at her mother's **A**, hitting it with the pinpoint accuracy of a Cy Young award winner. And she has an impressive imagination because of course she has to—Internet connection is spotty at the cottage, and they certainly can't afford cable. What's kind of weird, though, is that all of her imaginary playmates are actually imaginary foes: "She never created a friend, but seemed always to be sowing broadcast the dragon's teeth, whence sprung a harvest of armed enemies, against whom she rushed to battle."

Witnessing all of this behavior, her mother cries, Who the heck *are* you? Pearl responds, I am your Pearl. A perfectly reasonable answer.

Pearl would be justified to ask the same question of Hester. Because compared to the other parents of those days, who probably had "Spare the rod, spoil the child" carved on every available surface in their houses, Hester is a pretty chill mama. Besides, what would be the point of Hester even trying to discipline this kid, because Pearl has a sassy, capricious nature and a look that speaks volumes, and those volumes all say, Seriously, Ma, don't even waste your time, or mine.

Pearl's look also gives the impression of a "strange remoteness and intangibility: it was as if she were hovering in the air, and might vanish, like a glimmering light that comes we know not whence and goes we know not whither."

Between whither and whence, most of the time Hester is all, like, I'm sorry, is that my kid or is that some kind of mysterious sprite who could disappear at any moment? And if it is, could it maybe disappear for just half an hour so I can catch a quick nap, because I am *exhausted.*

But, here's the thing, Pearl sounds pretty darn cool, especially in comparison to all those sour, dour mini-Puritans who are running around: "...playing at going to church, perchance, or at scourging Quakers; or taking scalps in a sham fight with the Indians, or scaring one another with freaks of imitative witchcraft. Pearl saw, and gazed intently, but never sought to make acquaintance."

Yeah, Pearl, The Classics Slacker totally doesn't blame you for not wanting to hang out with kids whose idea of fun is pretending to pass around the collection plate after communion and doing rock-paper-scissors to decide who gets to play at whipping a member of a different Protestant sect first.

"Scourge the Quakers" has just got to be a euphemism, doesn't it?

And here's another unusual thing about Pearl—and it showed up when she was just a baby. Hawthorne suggests that while most infants first respond with delight to their mother's smile, this particular infant focused her rapt attention on something a little lower. You guessed it. The scarlet letter.

"One day, as her mother stooped over the cradle, the infant's eyes had been caught by the glimmering of the gold embroidery about the letter; and putting up her little hand she grasped at it, smiling, not doubtfully, but with a decided gleam....From that epoch, except when the child was asleep, Hester had never felt a moment's safety: not a moment's calm enjoyment of her."

Oy vey. Hester allows herself just a touch of bling and even that's way too much. Jeez.

Hawthorne chooses to end this particular chapter on an up note by adding another problem to Hester's already overflowing jar of pickles. One day she takes advantage of some quiet time to bestow a bit of early religious teaching on Pearl. She tells her that it was Baby Jesus' papa who sent her hither, i.e., to Earth. Pearl's response:

"He did not send me! I have no Heavenly Father!"

Wow! Pearl's not even an agnostic; she's gone full-on atheist by the age of, like, three. How is Hester going to deal with that kind of rebellion, which is *not* gonna fly where and when they live. Maybe she can just beg Pearl to keep the whole the-Universe-Is-without-Divinity-or-Design-because-It's-Just-a-Godless-Wasteland thing on the down-low.

8
DOES THIS SUIT OF ARMOR MAKE ME LOOK FAT?

In which a visit to the governor's residence makes Hester body-conscious

Hester has a plan to deliver gloves she embroidered to the governor in person so she can talk to him about another matter—a rumor going around that the townspeople want to take Pearl away from her. They have resolved that she's full of sin (may we once again direct your attention to the red letter **A** stitched on her dress) and thus, in all likelihood, the kid she has given birth to is a demon sprite. But maybe, they reason, Pearl's soul can be saved, *if* she is separated from Hester.

Hester has dressed up her daughter for the occasion in a "crimson velvet tunic of a peculiar cut, abundantly embroidered in fantasies and flourishes of gold thread."

Hey, what does that remind you of? Something someone else is wearing, maybe? No idea? Here, let Nate clue you in:

"It was the scarlet letter in another form: the scarlet letter endowed with life! The mother herself—as if the red ignominy were so deeply scorched into her brain that all her conceptions assumed its form—had carefully wrought out the similitude, lavishing many hours of morbid ingenuity to create an analogy between the object of her affection and the emblem of her guilt and torture."

Yikes, Nate, lighten up already! Have a yummy cocktail and maybe even go to Santa Barbara for a relaxing weekend. You're starting to sound a lot like a New England Puritan.

On the way to the mansion, mother and daughter encounter a posse of those annoying town kids. Hawthorne gives the children a line of dialogue that is so deliciously stilted, and probably so accurately conveys the lingo of the time, that The Classics Slacker just had to laugh out loud:

"Behold, verily, there is the woman of the scarlet letter: and of a truth, moreover, there is the likeness of the scarlet letter running along by her side! Come, therefore, and let us fling mud at them!"

Verily, indeed, kids! And forsooth, you wretched little punks, because Pearl is having none of it!

"But Pearl, who was a dauntless child, after frowning, stamping her foot, and shaking her little hand with a variety of threatening gestures, suddenly made a rush at the knot of her enemies, and put them all to flight. She resembled, in her fierce pursuit of them, an infant pestilence—the scarlet fever, or some such half-fledged angel of judgment—whose mission was to punish the sins of the rising generation."

You go, Pearl! Seriously, you know if this gal were living today, she'd be running for office somewhere, and The Classics Slacker would be the first person to sign up to phonebank for her campaign.

P.S. Between the eponymous letter and now the reference to

the fever of the same shade, if The Classics Slacker never reads or hears of the color "scarlet" (or, frankly, "crimson") again, it'll basically be too soon.

When Hester inquires of the governor's bond servant (read, essentially, "slave") if the governor is home, the servant tells her "Yea, his honorable worship is within. But he hath a godly minister or two with him, and likewise a leech."

(And you know it took The Classics Slacker a minute to remember that "leech" referred, at the time, to a doctor, on account of that lovely medical practice of bloodletting, and you know in that minute all The Classics Slacker could actually say was a very loud and a very drawn-out "EWWWWW!")

Even though the governor has company, the servant lets Hester in anyway. He's new to town and has never seen her scarlet letter and doesn't know her story. In fact, he's staring at the letter so intently that she wants to say, *Hey buddy, my eyes are up here*. He thinks she may be some "great lady," as if A stands for Aristocrat.

While waiting for the governor to become available, she and Pearl take the opportunity to roam around the entranceway. Grim-looking portraits of the governor's ancestors all seem to be passing judgment on her. Pearl ignores the portraits and instead runs toward a big ol' honking suit of armor. She tells Hester to look into the breast plate, which casts a reflection like a funhouse mirror.

"Hester looked by way of humoring the child; and she saw that, owing to the peculiar effect of this convex mirror, the scarlet letter was represented in exaggerated and gigantic proportions."

Wow, I had no idea it was that BIG. It's huge! It's like a friggin' Jumbotron! No wonder these judgmental Puritans are so over-the-top judgmental. I have got to lose a few pounds and shrink that puppy down a little.

Hester coaxes Pearl away from the flashy steel uniform and

into the garden, where Hawthorne takes a swipe at New England soil vis-à-vis the good earth of Merry Ol' England. But The Classics Slacker is not about to call Nate out on this prejudice because (a) it probably has a basis in science, and (b) it's not like The Classics Slacker is so rah-rah about this grim east coast burg that The Classics Slacker will be rushing to defend its flora and fauna anytime soon.

"Cabbages grew in plain sight; and a pumpkin-vine, rooted at some distance, had run across the intervening space, and deposited one of its gigantic products directly beneath the hall window, as if to warn the Governor that this great lump of vegetable gold was as rich an ornament as New England earth would offer him."

There are a few rose bushes around, and Pearl starts yelling about wanting one of the flowers just as the governor and his gaggle of grumpy goobers come walking down the path and, *Pearl,* shut your pie hole! Do you think these guys are going to find everything little kids do to be charming and make excuses all over the place for ill-behaved offspring? They're not a support group of wealthy divorced fathers in Beverly Hills, for goodness' sake!

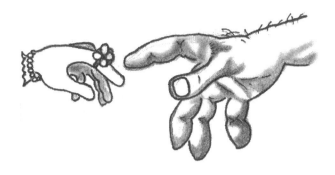

9
WHO'S YOUR DADDY?

In which Dimmesdale's relationship to Pearl is nearly revealed

When the guys break from their meeting, Hester stands ready to make her case for keeping Pearl. Side note: Of the four men present—Governor Bellingham, Pastor John Wilson, Reverend Arthur Dimmesdale, and Roger Chillingworth (whose name is always good for a snort, no?), she's been intimate with half of them.

And, as it turns out, her two love honeys have become somewhat intimate with each other, in that Chillingworth has become Dimmesdale's personal physician. Chillingworth's doctoring isn't helping much, though; ever since Hester's scaffold appearance, Dimmesdale's health has declined and he's continued to slide through ever-whitening shades of pale. Hmm, what might be causing that? Guilt, maybe?

Governor Bellingham and Mr. Wilson see Pearl before they encounter Hester, and Mr. Wilson declares: "What little bird of scarlet plumage may this be?" Ah yes, it's another name for Pearl, many of which are liberally sprinkled throughout the book (see Chart 1: "List of Names for Pearl" on page 37).

After referring to her as a member of the fowl family, Bellingham and Wilson start badgering the poor little kid about religion, for god's sake. At that point The Classics Slacker was really starting to see red (not scarlet and not crimson) on behalf of Pearl:

"Art thou a Christian child—ha? Dost know thy catechism? Or art thou one of those naughty elfs or fairies whom we thought to have left behind us, with other relics of Papistry, in merry old England?"

P.S. Isn't "elves" the plural of "elf"? Just sayin'.

When they see Hester, the real interrogation begins. Bellingham demands of Hester whether or not a fallen woman such as her would be the best person to raise an "immortal soul" like Pearl. And when Hester replies that she can teach her daughter what she has learned from "the red token" she is forced to wear, the governor says: "It is because of the stain which that letter indicates that we would transfer thy child to other hands."

Unlike The Classics Slacker, whose spewing of invective would have been volcanic at this point, Hester manages to contain herself. "This badge hath taught me—it daily teaches me—it is teaching me at this moment—lessons whereof my child may be the wiser and better." She says this without actually decking Bellingham, which, in The Classics Slacker's book, shows superhuman restraint.

Bellingham tells Wilson to interrogate the kid, and Wilson asks Pearl who made her, the correct answer being God, natch. Hester had tried to instruct her daughter about this most basic of religious tenets. But you know how feisty the young 'uns can be.

"After putting her finger in her mouth, with many ungracious refusals to answer good Mr. Wilson's question, the child finally announced that she had not been made at all, but had been plucked by her mother off the bush of wild roses that grew by the prison-door." Whoops! Sensing a serious blow to her case, Hester turns to Reverend Dimmesdale, who's doing his best impression of a snowdrift. She begs, "Speak for me! Thou knowest—for thou hast sympathies which these men lack—thou knowest what is in my heart." He knowest what's in anotherest body part, too. But no need to get into specifics here.

Although Dimmesdale's character is the very definition of milquetoast, he manages to make an impassioned and reasoned argument as to why Hester should keep Pearl.

And it works. The sullen men of state and church agree to leave Pearl in Hester's care. As long as she promises to keep her knees clenched and her knickers buttoned.

At that moment, Dimmesdale and Pearl "that wild and flighty little elf" (again, refer to Chart 1) share a sweet moment. She takes his hand and after a brief hesitation, he kisses her brow.

Chillingworth, who clearly can't stand to leave well enough alone, brings up that old chestnut about who's the dad of this kid: "Would it be beyond a philosopher's research, think ye, gentlemen, to analyze that child's nature, and, from it make a mould, to give a shrewd guess at the father?"

Unanimous reply from the gentlemen: Yes, it would. Way beyond.

Hester hightails it out of there with Pearl, and who can blame her? On the way out, she bumps into "Mistress Hibbins, Governor Bellingham's bitter-tempered sister and the same who, a few years later, was executed as a witch."

Wait, what? That's some heavy news to just casually drop into a one-sentence bio. It raises many questions. Didn't the governor have pardoning power? Or, worse, could he have pardoned her, but they were locked in the world's worst case of sibling rivalry? Or maybe he was out of office by then, too late to save her. We'll never know. If only Hawthorne had written a sequel: *Bellingham's Sister: She Was a Bitchy Witch, but Probably Didn't Deserve to Be Torched.*

Anyway, Mistress Hibbins, while she is still alive and well, has a tempting invitation for Hester: "Wilt thou go with us tonight? There will be a merry company in the forest; and I well-nigh promised the Black Man that comely Hester Prynne should make one."

And Hester's all, like, Not now, thanks, maybe later. "I must tarry at home and keep watch over my little Pearl."

Which raises yet another question. Who is the Black Man? Obviously not someone as entertaining as, say, Stevie Wonder. Hester definitely would have gotten a sitter to go see him.

Chart 1: List of Names for Pearl
airy sprite baby rhinoceros * bird of bright plumage bird of scarlet plumage demon offspring demon sprite elf-child flake of sea-foam flighty little elf humming-bird imp infant pestilence leprechaun little baggage Little Pearl (too many times to count) miniature demon sin-born child wild infant witch-baby woodland creature
*Okay, just kidding about this one, but she really is called all the others. All right, not "woodland creature," either. But all the others. Swear.

10
THE LEECH: GROSS!

In which...EWWWWW!

Right, so this chapter is all about Chillingworth, he of the off-kilter shoulders, who showed up in town just as Hester was being publicly shamed. And it has that swell title ("The Leech") because he was sort of a doctor and bloodletting with sucking aquatic parasites was state-of-the-art medicine back then. It would be as if today a doctor were referred to as "The Laser" or "The Angioplasty" or "The Prescription for Xanax."

Speaking of names, Hawthorne says we readers will remember that Roger Chillingworth first appeared on the scene with a different name. (We do? What was it? Smokey Rogersworth? Ace Worthington?) But he decided that his old name should nevermore be spoken, as it was connected to his life as Hester's husband back in the old country. He doesn't want his true identity associated with the town trollop: "He resolved not to be pilloried beside her on her pedestal of shame." Chivalry, if not dead at this point, is clearly on life support.

Thus the doctor formerly known as Smokey or Ace joins the medical group in town, which has an apothecary and a surgeon who uses a razor (ouch!!!!). They could really use an anesthesiologist in the practice. And definitely a female gynecologist, but that's asking way too much for 1642.

In any case, the citizen in town who most urgently needs medical attention is the Rev. Arthur Dimmesdale. If he loses any more color, the townspeople will be able to see through to the back of his head. "With every successive Sabbath, his cheek was paler and thinner, and his voice more tremulous than before. Was he weary of his labors? Did he wish to die?" Maybe. So the townsfolk are super psyched that Chillingworth, aka Dr. Leech, has come to town. Maybe he can heal their beloved minister before he becomes completely translucent.

But Dimmesdale, fading by the minute, maintains that he doesn't need a doctor. *I just need a few stiff drinks; I just need to get laid. Oh Hes-ter!* But he can't say that out loud, of course. Instead, he tells Chillingworth that if God wants him to perish, so be it. But Chillingworth says that God would want him to recover and continue his work. You can hardly argue with that. Well, you could, but why would you?

Chillingworth's take on what God wants prevails, and he becomes the reverend's attending physician—his leech, if you will. Shortly thereafter, Dr. Bloodsucking Worms takes the practice of house calls a little too seriously and actually moves in with his pale patient. But instead of feeling stifled, Dimmesdale enjoys the company of his new roommate. It's the conversation he likes best. Chillingworth offers him a different perspective than the religious scholars he normally hangs out with:

"It was as if a window were thrown open, admitting a freer atmosphere into the close and stifled study, where his life was wasting itself away, amid lamp-light, or obstructed day-beams, and the musty fragrance, be it sensual or moral, that exhales from books."

Whoa! This guy feels deeply! If this is how he's affected by sharing quarters with Chillingworth, what was it like getting carnal with Hester?

Chillingworth finds the arrangement to his liking, too, but for a different reason: "He deemed it essential, it would seem, to know the man, before attempting to do him good. Roger Chillingworth…strove to go deep into his patient's bosom, delving among his principles, prying into his recollections, and probing everything with a cautious touch, like a treasure-seeker in a dark cavern."

Wow, it's almost as though this bloodsucking worm might think there's something else going on beneath that sickly, pious surface, huh?

Anyway, when news spreads that these two have moved in together, "there was much joy throughout the town." (You know there isn't much that jollies up these people.) It's only slightly less wonderful than if Reverend Dimmesdale had finally settled down with a nice young virgin—"one of the many blooming damsels, spiritually devoted to him, to become his devoted wife" (that's a lot of devotion)—which the whole town would love to see.

But the reverend is all, like, Thanks, I'm good: "He rejected all suggestions of the kind, as if priestly celibacy were one of his articles of Church discipline." *As if?* Meaning it *isn't* a rule? Then why is he so bent out of shape over his nooky-nook with Hester?

Everything's looking rosy (note: not scarlet and not crimson and not red, just rosy) among the townspeople, happy as they are that the members of the We-Did-It-with-Hester Club are living together. But you know it can't stay that way for long.

Sure enough, some of the townspeople, who really have very little to do, start to think that Chillingworth is sketchy. They think he looks different since he moved in with Dimmesdale. Whereas before "his expression had been calm, meditative, scholar-like. Now there was something ugly and evil in his face..."

Oh what could be causing this transformation? The Classics Slacker doesn't know...maybe...**SATAN?????!!!!!**

A totally reasonable conjecture as it turns out. "It grew to be a widely diffused opinion that the Rev. Arthur Dimmesdale... was haunted either by Satan himself or Satan's emissary, in the guise of old Roger Chillingworth. This diabolical agent had the Divine permission, for a season, to burrow into the clergyman's intimacy, and plot against his soul." God and Satan sometimes work together? Who knew?

Beyond loathing his ugly, evil devil face, some people have another beef with Chillingworth. They question "the relations betwixt Mr. Dimmesdale and the mysterious old physician."

Relations? Wait a minute...could it be...omg...are they **GAY???!!!** Satan and witches and the Black Man would all be invited over for dinner at one of the respectable homes in the village sooner than a couple of gay men would be accepted in the Land of Intolerance.

Run, guys, run! Before they string you up on the scaffold!

11

LOCKED AND GOADED

In which not even a leech can suck a secret out of Dimmesdale

Chillingworth is certain that Dimmesdale is harboring a secret, and he is determined to pry it out of him, even if he has to use a scalpel. "He now dug into the poor clergyman's heart, like a miner searching for gold; or, rather, like a sexton delving into a grave, possibly in quest of a jewel that had been buried on the dead man's bosom." Or like a plumber unclogging a toilet. Or like a dog digging up a bone. Or like…well, you get the idea.

Something about all this digging has a weirdo effect on Chillingworth's peepers. A "light glimmered out of the physician's eyes, burning blue and ominous, like the reflection of a furnace." Or like the revolving blue lights of a police cruiser. Or like neon beams glinting off a disco ball. Or like…well, you get the idea. Chilly is the one who could use some doctoring, specifically from a gifted ophthalmologist.

Dimmy must be alarmed by Chilly's strange new electromagnetic eyeballs, but he manages to look past them, and the two men settle down for a lengthy discussion on the subject of secrets.

Dimmy: Maybe I'm wanting to reveal a secret but maybe I'm just not able to.

Chilly: Wouldn't it feel better to just tell me your secret, like, maybe right now?

Dimmy: Nuh uh, don't think I can, but, yeah, I get your point because a lot of people have confessed their sins to me on their deathbeds.

Chilly: Okay, so then why not just blurt your sins out to me ASAP?

The Classics Slacker has to confess that The Classics Slacker's hand found itself unconsciously making that "yap, yap, yap" gesture where you bring your four fingers to tap your thumb in rapid succession because the back and forth between these two guys went on for-like-*ever*.

Mercifully, the endless patter was interrupted by the sound of Hester and Pearl playing in the graveyard next door because apparently there are no parks or recreation centers in that dreary town.

The men look out the window to see Pearl literally *dancing on a grave,* and her mother tells her to knock it off with the shenanigans already. At that point Pearl finds some prickly burrs and "arranged them along the lines of the scarlet letter that decorated the maternal bosom…Hester did not pluck them off." Because when Hawthorne goes for imagery, he likes to keep it understated.

Well, the guys start talkin' smack about the kid (Chillingworth: "What, in heaven's name, is she? Is the imp altogether evil? Hath she affections? Hath she any discoverable principle of being?" Dimmesdale: "Whether capable of good, I know not.").

Pearl sees them up in the window looking down on her and

her mother, so she "threw one of the prickly burrs at the Rev. Mr. Dimmesdale. The sensitive clergyman shrank, with nervous dread, from the light missile. Detecting his emotion, Pearl clapped her little hands in the most extravagant ecstasy."

And The Classics Slacker must once again cheer, You go, Pearl! Girl, please be a real person and please grow up and please run for office and please let The Classics Slacker be your campaign manager because you rock with your I-Will-Not-Put-up-with-Being-Dissed attitude!

After Hester and Pearl leave, the two roomies resume their chat about secrets, because Chillingworth is like a freakin' terrier with a bone on this. But the discussion is significantly shorter this time and Chillingworth changes the subject to that of Dimmesdale's health. The reverend says, Give it to me straight, Doc, and Chillingworth is all, like, Pal, you got it bad and that ain't good. Of course, the Leech grabs this chance to ask once again: Why not just tell me what deep, dark secret is eating away at your spirit 'n' your flesh 'n' stuff?

In response, the suffering clergyman musters a burst of energy and says, I'll confess to God and no one else, you putz, so back it all the way off! Or words to that effect.

And then Dimmy falls sound asleep in his chair over something he had been reading—almost certainly the "Introductory to The Scarlet Letter." That's when Chilly comes in and opens the reverend's shirt. What is revealed on Dimmy's chest makes Chilly's dark little heart skip for joy. The Classics Slacker isn't entirely sure what the Leech saw, but The Classics Slacker is guessing it wasn't an exceptionally large and garish tattoo of the name "Shirley" in a florid font with a big heart in place of the dot on top of the "i" that the reverend doesn't remember getting during a drunken weekend in Vegas, because that would be far too much fun.

But whatever it is, it has to be something wicked intense:

"Had a man seen old Roger Chillingworth, at that moment of his ecstasy, he would have had no need to ask how Satan comports himself when a precious human soul is lost to heaven, and won into his kingdom."

The Classics Slacker hears ya, Mr. Hawthorne! Because is invoking the specter of Beelzebub himself a great harbinger of gloom and doom, or what?

12
ONE PLUS ONE EQUALS THREE

*In which Dimmesdale's failed attempts to confess his sins
only make him more lovable*

Our guy Dimmesdale is having a heck of a bad time on several fronts. First, there's his roommate. It isn't that Chillingworth drinks his beer and doesn't replace it. The problem is that Chillingworth now knows Dimmesdale's secret and has been using the information to torment the poor reverend more than ever. He's a dastardly doctor, a loathsome leech, a foul physician, an awful apothecary, a hateful healer, a mangy medic, a sucky specialist—

Help! The Classics Slacker can't stop alliterating!

Deep breaths, deep breaths…

Okay, The Classics Slacker is back.

In short, Chillingworth is such a dickhead. "He became, thenceforth, not a spectator only, but a chief actor in the poor minister's interior world. He could play upon him as he chose.

Would he arouse him with a throb of agony? The victim was for ever on the rack; it needed only to know the spring that controlled the engine:—and the physician knew it well." Or he can go the fear route, using dark magic to produce grisly phantoms that surround the clergyman and point their fingers at him.

You know we've all had *that* roommate.

Enduring the antics of a live-in tormentor would satisfy the most guilt-ridden of clergymen's need for penance. But Dimmesdale wants more:

"In Mr. Dimmesdale's secret closet, under lock and key, there was a bloody scourge. Oftentimes, this Protestant and Puritan divine had plied it on his own shoulders; laughing bitterly at himself the while, and smiting so much the more pitilessly because of that bitter laugh."

Indeed, it's the bitter laugh that gives self-torture an extra special zing. But really, what a sick pup! It was just sex, Dimmy! It's not like you were caught stealing office supplies! Put down the whip and stop beating yourself up (literally).

Ironically, the guilt and torment and agita that he's wallowing in makes Dimmesdale's celebrity rise. He advances beyond other clergymen with more experience and becomes an A-lister (ha!). Those guys had everything except "heaven's last and rarest attestation of their office, the Tongue of Flame." Ouch! That's spicy! Does that mean that our own pale preacher *does* have the Tongue of Flame? Did Hester know about his hot tongue before she let him explore her underworld?

But back to Dimmy's increasing fame. The church people uniformly think he's dreamy. And the I-Am-Ever-Writhing-Internally-and-Externally-under-the-Burden-of-My-Horrible-Sinfulness persona seems to be quite irresistible to the ladies. The virgins, in particular, grow weak and wobbly kneed around him. The old people think he's not healthy and that he's going up to heaven before they will, so they are all trying to reserve grave plots near his. He's more sought after than a parking spot in midtown Manhattan.

The more he tells his flock that he's a sinner—and not just any sinner but "a viler companion of the vilest, the worst of sinners, an abomination, a thing of unimaginable iniquity"—the more they love him. He's, like, What more can I say to make them understand? "Could there be plainer speech than this?" Well, yeah. Maybe if he said, *Okay you guys, remember Hester? Prynne? The lady with the red A? I'm the guy she A'd with. And if you are not getting it, here's a chart to help you see it. It was I who didst hitteth that. Now all you virgins, sit up and stop fainting!*

Sigh, if only. Another sermon ends and our sad-sack, sickly pastor goes home with nothing to look forward to except another evening of scourging, followed by nightly vigils wherein "his brain often reeled, and visions seemed to flit before him." Dead Mom, dead Dad, dead friends, flocks of angels, herds of elephants, dancing hippos, bucket-carrying brooms…oh wait, that's *Fantasia*.

Fortunately, Dimmesdale knows none of these visions are real. They aren't "solid in their nature, like yonder table of carved oak, or that big, square, leathern-bound and brazen-clasped volume of divinity" or that drinking glass placed upon thine nightstand or that stately chest of drawers containing all thine underwear or that hygienically sealed animal-skinned condom in thy leathern wallet ye should have used when ye layeth down with the corporeal Hester Prynne.

Oh, will this torment ever cease? And then, at last, "a new thought had struck him." Ouch! Could it work?

Instead of stripping down for a good scourging sesh, Dimmy dresses up in his Sunday best, "as if it had been for public worship, and precisely in the same manner." Then he's outta the house, into the night, and loose on the streets! The Classics Slacker can't wait to find out what happens next!

13

I LOVE THE NIGHTLIFE,
I GOT TO BOOGIE,
ON THE SCAFFOLD, OW

In which some weird stuff goes down upon the stage of shame

Suffering from cabin fever and assorted other fevers, Dimmesdale decides to go for a midnight walk to clear his mind. He heads straight for the scaffold where Hester served her three-hour public sentence and actually climbs up onto it. All of a sudden, he lets out a shriek. *Oops, now I've gone and done it.* "The whole town will awake, and hurry forth, and find me here!" And they will finally see that he's a no-good, low-down, ding-dang sinner.

But the whole town doesn't awaken. Only Governor Bellingham and his witchy sister Mistress Hibbins turn on their lamps. But they soon extinguish them, chalking up the sound to witches "whose voices at that period, were often heard to pass over the settlements or lonely cottages, as they rode with Satan through the air." Right, no biggie. Only flying witches, riding with the Devil. If you hear 'em, you can just roll over and go back to sleep.

Dimmesdale continues his nocturnal scaffold-stand, alone except for witches whizzing over his head. But not for long. Because, look, there's a light coming down the street! Wow, this town is buzzing more than Times Square on a Saturday night! It's Reverend Wilson fresh from the deathbed of Governor Winthrop, followed by Hester and Pearl also returning from that same deathbed. Hester was taking funeral robe measurements and Pearl was, uh, experiencing the worst 'Take Your Kid to Work Day' ever? Bringing up the rear of the Winthrop death-bed parade is our own Chillingworth, who didn't have anything left to do for the governor, but it was clearly *the* place to be that evening. Indeed, is there anyone left in town who *wasn't* at the deathbed of Governor Winthrop?

Wilson walks right past the scaffold without noticing Dimmesdale, who starts to feel the chill of the night air stiffening his limbs and—weakling that he is—imagines that he won't be able to climb down. In the morning, the townspeople will discover his frozen body there, not just all the old folks, of course, but also those hot, young babes in the congregation with their hot, pale knockers:

"The young virgins who so idolized their minister, and had made a shrine for him in their white bosoms, which now, by-the-bye, in their hurry and confusion, they would scantly have given themselves time to cover with their kerchiefs." Hawthorne, take a cold shower, bro. Your morality tale is starting to veer into Puritan porn.

Dimmesdale, going a little nuts at this point, starts laughing that loud, crazy laugh that calls to mind hyenas braying to be heard over chainsaws. That sound is met with the contrapunto of "a light, airy, childish laugh" belonging to Pearl, who's coming down the street with her mama.

Cheerful helloes are exchanged all around, and Dimmesdale has the polished elm cojones to ask Hester to join him up on the scaffold that she no doubt holds in such fond memory. He says he didn't stand with her there the last time, so he wants to do it now, in the dark, with no one watching, seven years after the fact. Surely one of the worst cases of too little, too late in the history of literature.

But Hester joins him up there anyway and Dimmesdale holds her hand and Pearl's. He's loving the feeling of his little family joined in this way. "The three formed an electric chain." Which would be convenient if any of the villagers' car batteries needed a jump.

Pearl thinks this family togetherness stuff is all well and good but asks him point-blank if he'll assume the same hand-holding formation in broad daylight.

You wanna guess what Dimmesdale's response is? If this comes as *any* surprise, you haven't been paying attention…

"Nay; not so, my little Pearl. I shall, indeed, stand with thy mother and thee one other day, but not to-morrow."

Such a weenie this guy is.

At this point, Hawthorne clearly decided that his book was starting to drag (at least, this is The Classics Slacker's supposition). Time to toss in an astronomical pyrotechnic display. Dimmesdale looks up and sees, what is that? A bird? A plane? No, it's a huge scarlet letter A, formed either by a meteor or a speck of dust in his eyeball.

While all this is going on, Dimmesdale notices Chillingworth lurking (Seriously, was the verb "to lurk" created for this guy, or what?) not far away. He asks Hester who that awful guy is ("I have a nameless horror of the man!"). Silly goose, she says, can't you tell it's your roommate/doctor who has been examining you up and down and crosswise for the last several months? Well,

51

yes, of course Dimmy knows who Chilly *is;* he just wants to know *who* he is. But Hester is mute on this point as she had promised not to give up Chilly as her husband. Not that this bit of intelligence would make one whit of difference to anyone.

Chilly steps to the foreground and explains what he's doing there. He was at Governor Winthrop's deathbed (yeah, we know) and was heading home when he saw light on the scaffold. Then he convinces Dimmesdale to go home with him to their bachelor pad. "Come with me, I beseech you, Reverend sir, else you will be poorly able to do Sabbath duty to-morrow."

Turns out to be good advice as the next day—Sunday— Dimmy delivers one humdinger of a sermon, "a discourse which was held to be the richest and most powerful, and the most replete with heavenly influences, that had ever proceeded from his lips."

The reverend is feeling pretty good about himself until…the church sexton tells him that he found his black glove that morning "on the scaffold where evil-doers are set up to public shame."

Busted! But before Dimmesdale even has a chance to defend himself, the sexton comes up with a perfectly plausible explanation: "Satan dropped it there, I take it, intending a scurrilous jest against your reverence."

Yep, that Satan, such a cutup.

14
ALTERNATIVE ADJECTIVES

*In which Hester's letter has come to stand for lots of other **A** words*

Hester has been a fixture in town for so long that the locals have practically forgotten what her red letter **A** represents. It's partly because she's spent a good bit of the seven years since her conviction tending to the poor. She serves them food and darns their socks and offers up her "breast" (as Hawthorne calls it), which despite being covered with a "badge of shame" serves as a nice soft pillow "for the head that needed one."

Of course, there is danger in putting your face full upon Hester's breast. You could wind up with a big ol' **A**-shaped line on your cheek. But for those who seek comfort from Hester, it's a small price to pay. Everyone loves her so much that "many people refused to interpret the scarlet **A** by its original signification. They said it meant Able; so strong was Hester Prynne, with a woman's strength."

Well, isn't that convenient? "Able" starts with **A**, and that letter is already attached to Hester's chest! It's a seamless transition isn't it! And The Classics Slacker bets Hester is so gracious and forgiving, she probably welcomes this change with humility and gratitude.

(The Classics Slacker, meanwhile, would like to suggest to those long-dead fictional townspeople that they go right ahead and slap a big ol' A on their own chests, which stands for...well you can guess it isn't Able or even Absorbent.)

It's not just the poor and middle-class townspeople who are coming around to the view that Hester is A-okay. Remember the rich people who bought her extravagant fashions? Demand remains high. To those who can afford an original Prynne, her A stands for Absolutely Fabulous. Others, a large group of extremely gullible townspeople, believe that Hester's A gives her a superpower. "It was reported, and believed by many, that an Indian had drawn an arrow against the badge, and that the missile struck it, but fell harmless to the ground." In this case, A stands for Arrow-proof.

But here's a question. Why in holy heck were Indians shooting her? Did they want her to hand over Pearl, the most interesting character in the book? Did they want her to design a collection of leather-fringed suits free of charge for next year's Thanksgiving? Did they want her to go into business with them in a charming little shop downtown that sells high-end turquoise handicrafts and organic clover honey at exorbitant prices? The Classics Slacker thinks Hawthorne missed a chance for an exciting chapter by dismissing this entire Indian arrow-shooting incident in a single sentence.

Too bad. Instead, the next thing Hawthorne tell us is that even those pissy old magistrates are joining Team Hester: "Day by day...their sour and rigid wrinkles were relaxing into something which, in the due course of years, might grow to be an expression of almost benevolence." Take your time, guys.

Hester herself is Alarmed—over the state of Reverend Dimmesdale. She saw him up close during their midnight rendezvous on the scaffold and even in the dark she was "shocked at the condition to which she found the clergyman reduced." In other words, he's a wreck. "His nerve seemed absolutely destroyed. His moral force was abased into more than childish weakness."

Right away she figures out what his problem is. While she's been wearing an A and tending to the poor and enjoying an increasingly favored reputation in town, he's been suffering under the burden of their Big Secret, while being venerated as a virtuous pastor.

Hester could justifiably say to Dimmesdale, "Well, sucks to be you," and leave him bereft on the street. But no...our main character, who is as saintly as Mother Theresa (but far less wrinkled), feels she owes Dimmesdale something.

"Hester saw—or seemed to see—that there lay a responsibility upon her in reference to the clergyman, which she owed to no other, nor to the whole world besides....Here was the iron link of mutual crime, which neither he nor she could break. Like all other ties, it brought along with it its obligations."

Okay, let's see, Hester. So you two danced between the sheets. And that was, like, so highly forbidden in your uptight society that it even gave rise to the word *puritanical*. And because of that no-no you committed *together*—despite the fact that he hasn't ever admitted his guilt and has left you to bear the punishment all on your own and has not done one thing to help you for all these years (not one scarlet cent of child support)—*you* are on the hook to help *him* with *his* suffering while he basically gets a free ride vis-à-vis everyone else? That about the size of it?

Wow, Hester. If you could just hang on until circa 1970s Boston, you could attend a few women's consciousness-raising groups. Burn thy corset and march for equal rights. You need it. Badly.

Finally, Hawthorne ends the chapter with a teaser followed by a cliffhanger that left The Classics Slacker wondering if Nate had studied story structure with the *Law and Order* franchise writers.

Teaser: Hester will confront Chillingworth, the man formerly known as her spouse and Dimmesdale's roommate/tormentor, because she is stronger now than she was on that night years ago when she promised the Leech she wouldn't divulge his identity.

Cliffhanger: "The occasion was not long to seek. One afternoon, walking with Pearl in a retired part of the peninsula, she beheld the old physician with a basket on one arm and a staff in the other hand, stooping along the ground in quest of roots and herbs to concoct his medicine withal."

Okay, so as far as teasers and cliffhangers go, these ain't much, unless you are just waking up from a nap. But we're more than halfway through, so we might as well forge onward at this point. Like our heroine, The Classics Slacker is no quitter.

15

BEAUTY AND THE BEAST

*In which Beauty wears a red letter and the
Beast is a red-eyed devil*

Previously on *The Classics Slacker Reads The Scarlet Letter,*
Hester spotted Chillingworth digging for roots and shoots
and fruits to make his creepy medicines. Deciding this is the perfect opportunity to talk to him, she sends Pearl off to the water's
edge to play. "So the child flew away like a bird, and, making bare
her small white feet, went pattering along the moist margin of
the sea."

Pearl quickly conjures up an imaginary friend who looks
exactly like her and challenges the "visionary little maid" to a
race. But the imaginary friend suggests a frolic in the water instead and Pearl likes that idea better. Pearl doesn't do anything
half-assed.

Anyway, Hester turns her attention to Chillingworth. *Oh,
yoo-hoo,* she says, *yonder gatherer of herbs, physician leech guy,*

I'd like a word with you. He says okay and she tells him that Reverend Dimmesdale ain't looking so great, and as she says so, she notices that Chilly also has two strange new afflictions to go along with his irregular shoulders. His eyes are red, and he's puffing out smoke.

"Ever and anon there came a glare of red light out of his eyes; as if the old man's soul were on fire, and kept on smouldering duskily within his breast, until, by some casual puff of passion, it was blown into a momentary flame." Forget scarlet letters, this guy has scarlet eyes. And he's breathing fire. What's going on? "In a word, old Roger Chillingworth was a striking evidence of man's faculty of transforming himself into a devil."

Oh, that explains it.

Let it be known that if The Classics Slacker had encountered a man-turned-devil out on a desolate beach, The Classics Slacker would've rushed to the water's edge, gathered up Pearl, and hightailed it out of there. Heck, The Classics Slacker might've left Pearl behind; that little girl can fend for herself. But Hester doesn't scare easily (her A-emblazoned chest deflects arrows, after all). She's on a mission to figure out from Chillingworth what's wrong with Dimmesdale, and she will not be deterred, never mind that her former husband has turned into a coal-burning furnace.

The two of them start chatting as Hester waves the smoke away. Their conversation begins amicably. Chillingworth tells her that the elders have discussed commuting her sentence and that he supports the idea 110 percent: "Yonder scarlet letter might be taken off your bosom. On my life, Hester, I make my entreaty to the worshipful magistrate that it might be done forthwith."

But instead of falling to her knees in gratitude, Hester replies that it's not up to those dudes to decide. "Were I worthy to be quit of it, it would fall away of its own nature." Worthy or no, that sucker isn't going anywhere because she stitched it on but good, and you know the seam ripper hasn't been invented yet that could pull it off. She allows for the possibility that if she be "transformed into something that should speak a different purport" of it, that would be okay. Like if the town opened a Pilgrim's Playhouse and she won all the leading Actress roles.

Hester puts the A subject Aside and starts in on what she came to say. How Dimmesdale is deteriorating both because she and Chillingworth are withholding the secret of their marriage and because Chillingworth has been torturing him.

"You tread behind his every footstep. You are beside him, sleeping and waking. You search his thoughts. You burrow and rankle in his heart! Your clutch is on his life, and you cause him to die daily a living death, and still he knows you not. In permitting this I have surely acted a false part by the only man to whom the power was left me to be true!"

Chillingworth immediately ups the ante and tells Hester that ol' Dimmesdale would be dead by now if not for his help. "The richest fee that ever physician earned from monarch could not have bought such care as I have wasted on this miserable priest," he says. But Hester is having none of it...Death would be a step up for the poor schmuck, Doc. So step back, Jack!

Hester then goes *way* negative, and seriously, who could blame her? She tells Chillingworth she *has* to tell Dimmesdale who Chillingworth actually is (her former husband, in case you've stopped following along), and if that means Chillingworth is going to reveal Dimmesdale's guilt to everyone, so be it. It's not like things don't already suck anyway.

"Do with him as thou wilt!" she says. "There is no good for him, no good for me, no good for thee! There is no good for little Pearl! There is no path to guide us out of this dismal maze!"

[Cue Elvis: *We're caught in a trap...I can't walk out...Because I love you too much, baby*]

And you know what's kind of creepy? Chillingworth actually gets a little turned on by Hester's "Ohh, what's the point" attitude. He was "unable to restrain a thrill of admiration too; for there was a quality almost majestic in the despair which she expressed."

Eyeing her up and down, he says: "Thou hadst great elements." Ah yes, he remembers her elements most fondly. Historical fact: Complimenting a woman's elements was an oft-used Puritan pickup line.

Hester so doesn't fall for it. Before she leaves, she has one more suggestion for Chillingworth: to forgive her and Dimmesdale. If he can, his eyes might return to a color more resembling a human's. Alas, Chillingworth says he doesn't possess that kind of power; he's just fortune's fool. He actually says "fate," but it's so much cooler to quote Shakespeare when you have the opportunity. Oh, and he says he's down with her revealing his identity to Dimmesdale. So that's a bonus.

Overall, a good meeting.

Which of course means things can only go downhill from here.

16
BIRDS DO IT, BEES DO IT

In which Hester and Pearl have "the talk," sort of

As Hester watches Chillingworth walk away, she's feeling miffed. *I gave you the best years of my life, you ugly old cuss,* she mutters to herself. *And what did it get me? A whole lotta nuttin.* She no longer feels as if she deserved her punishment. In that moment, she's just p.o.'d to the max.

Suddenly she remembers that she left her kid by the water's edge. Whew! She's still there. No harm done. Pearl's just been playing with rocks and shells and Portuguese man-o-wars. "She made little boats out of birch-bark, and freighted them with snail-shells, and sent out more ventures on the mighty deep than any merchant in New England..."

Hey! Little kids of today! Are you hearing this? Pearl's in Puritan New England in the seventeenth century, and she's keeping herself entertained all on her own. She's not just imaginative, she's enterprising. So put down your smartphones and start thinking and creating for yourselves. (Unless of course you are reading *The Classics Slacker Reads The Scarlet Letter* on said smartphone.) Maybe make some swell fashions while you're at it, just like Pearl did:

"Her final employment was to gather seaweed of various kinds, and make herself a scarf or mantle, and a head-dress, and thus assume the aspect of a little mermaid. She inherited her mother's gift for devising drapery and costume. As the last touch to her mermaid's garb, Pearl took some eel-grass and imitated, as best she could, on her own bosom the decoration with which she was so familiar on her mother's. A letter—the letter A—but freshly green instead of scarlet."

You know Hawthorne had to be thinking *The Chartreuse Letter, A Sequel.*

Hester calls Pearl over and sees her miniature green A. She would have done well to ignore it. Instead, she's amused and asks Pearl if she knows what the A stands for. (Amphibian? Australian? Al dente?)

Sure I do, Mom! You know how Reverend Dimmesdale is always covering his chest with his hand? It has something to do with that.

Uhhh ohhh…The kid has linked her with the reverend somehow, and now Hester desperately wants to know if Pearl understands the down and dirty details of what happens when two people love each other very much.

She even thinks that if Pearl somehow holds that level of knowledge, she might be able to lean on her daughter as a trusted friend, something she hasn't had in, well, never. She's never had a friend, much less a trusted one.

Hester is truly losing it here. Pearl is seven, not seventeen. Even if she were older, it's considered very bad parenting indeed to use your child as a confidante. To that, The Classics Slacker says, without question, eww.

It's a moot point. Upon further questioning, Hester discovers that Pearl is just babbling nonsensically, as kids will do. But because her mom has brought up the subject, now she demands to know what the scarlet letter stands for. *What does it mean, Mom? What? What? What? What? What?*

When she doesn't receive an answer, she just keeps on going: "But in good earnest now, mother dear, what does this scarlet letter mean?—and why dost thou wear it on thy bosom? and why does the minister keep his hand over his heart?"

Seriously, Ma, what's the 411 on this whole letter A thing? For reals this time, 'kay?

Well, mama's had it about up to here, so she applies that surefire formula of lying to make the kid shut up: "Silly Pearl, what questions are these? There are many things in this world that a child must not ask about. What know I of the minister's heart? And as for the scarlet letter, I wear it for the sake of its gold thread."

It's the thread, kid, okay? The thread is gold and I like gold and the letter has nothing to do with ADULTERY, so get that right outta your head, got it?

Well, of course you know how much little kids savor repetition, and how much they won't let things go? Like, they hear the same joke a bazillion times and still laugh as much at the punchline as the first time and then demand to hear it again and again?

All of which is to say that of course Pearl wakes up the next morning and starts the whole interrogation all over again:

"Mother!—Mother!—Why does the minister keep his hand over his heart?"

Okay, that is IT, kid!

"Hold thy tongue, naughty child! Do not tease me; else I shall put thee into the dark closet!"

You hear that, Pearl? You wanna know from Puritan pedagogy? Mama gonna *show* you some Puritan pedagogy!

17

AIN'T NO SUNSHINE

In which Hester, now shunned even by the sun,
schemes to bump into Dimmesdale "by accident"

Hester is hot to find Dimmesdale ASAP and warn him about Chillingworth. She could head for the reverend's office where lots of parishioners go to unburden themselves, but she won't do that. Why? Because (a) you never know where that miserable leech is going to come slithering in (or however it is that leeches ambulate) and (b) we must have wide-open spaces because nothing less will contain all this stuff we got goin' on between us, right, Rev?

"She would need the whole wide world to breathe in, while they talked together—for all these reasons Hester never thought of meeting him in any narrower privacy than beneath the open sky."

Hester figures out a plan for when she can be out walking casually and intersect with Dimmesdale in that adorable Oh,-

Reverend!-How-Funny-that-We-Should-Both-Be-Here-at-the-Same-Time-and-the-Same-Place way that every rom-com demands.

At last the opportunity arises. "She learnt that he had gone, the day before, to visit the Apostle Eliot, among his Indian converts. He would probably return by a certain hour in the afternoon of the morrow. Betimes, therefore, the next day, Hester took little Pearl—who was necessarily the companion of all her mother's expeditions, however inconvenient her presence—and set forth."

Of course it's a pain to bring Pearl. Unfortunately, there's no way around it. There's no Ye Olde Daycare Centre in town for dropping kids off.

As mom and daughter wait for Dimmesdale to come traipsing through the woods, Pearl—ever observant and ever using her words as daggers in a way that belies her youth—notes that there ain't no sunshine when Hester's around and what's that all about?

"The sunshine does not love you, Mother," she says. *It runs and hides behind the clouds whenever you show up because of that scarlet letter A on your bosom, which I'm now guessing stands for Average.* "Stand you here, and let me run and catch it. I am but a child. It will not flee from me—for I wear nothing on my bosom yet!"

Ouch!

Despite her daughter talkin' smack, Hester enjoys seeing Pearl aglow in the sunshine. But then she hopes that it won't be all bright days and roses for her kid because—The Classics Slacker is guessing—that would make for a superficial character who would fit into a remake of *Beverly Hills 90210* more than a classic novel:

"She wanted—what some people want throughout life— a grief that should deeply touch her, and thus humanize and make her capable of sympathy. But there was time enough yet for little Pearl."

Yeah, plenty o' time, Hester. Sheesh. Enjoy the nice weather for a few minutes, huh, and give the *Ohh, no, what if my daughter gets too easy a ride through life?* a rest, yeah? Because, seriously, what are the odds of that happening when you're constantly surrounded by dour freakin' *Puritans?*

Hester tells Pearl to sit with her while they wait, and Pearl says she will, but only if Hester tells her a story about the Black Man. Because you know how kids are with demanding to be bribed into cooperating or else they'll have one of those charming tantrums they're so famous for.

Hester's wondering where Pearl even heard about the Black Man in the first place, and Pearl tells her from that kooky Mistress Hibbins, the sister of the governor. The one who's a witch, you remember:

"She said that a thousand and a thousand people had met him here, and had written in his book, and have his mark on them. And that ugly tempered lady, old Mistress Hibbins, was one. And, mother, the old dame said that this scarlet letter was the Black Man's mark on thee, and that it glows like a red flame when thou meetest him at midnight, here in the dark wood. Is it true, mother? And dost thou go to meet him in the nighttime?"

See, this is where a nice educational program like *Sesame Street* and a television to watch it on would come in handy to keep children away from practitioners of the dark arts. But since that's all a few centuries away, Hester tells Pearl, Yeah, okay, fine, I once met the Black Man and "this scarlet letter is his mark!" and can we please just *drop* it now?

Hester sees Dimmesdale draw near and he does not look good. Pearl is hoping the approaching figure is the Black Man because she's dying to meet him, as if he's Barack Obama. Hester tells Pearl to scram, but not to go too far and to come back when she is called. Apparently Hester isn't the least bit concerned about

Pearl encountering the Black Man out there. She's out to capture a man of her own.

But is this the best she can do?

"He looked haggard and feeble, and betrayed a nerveless despondency in his air. There was a listlessness in his gait, as if he saw no reason for taking one step further, nor felt any desire to do so, but would have been glad, could he be glad of anything, to fling himself down at the root of the nearest tree, and lie there passive for evermore."

Yikes! Somebody get this poor guy a Starbucks triple venti grande espresso with a double shot of Red Bull, stat!

18
THE PUPPET AND HIS PUPPETEER

*In which Hester inexplicably props up that
whiny weenie man of the cloth*

Dimmesdale is walking through the woods, alone, despondent, contemplating lying down and dying among the leaves when Hester calls to him: *Oh, Reverend Dimmesdale! Arthur! Yoo-hoo! It's Hester! I'm over here down yonder!* He hears her voice, sees her, and asks: "Is it thou? Art thou in life?" And Hester's, like, Yeah, and asks, What about you, "dost thou yet live?"

And The Classics Slacker is, like, What's with all the questions? Did either of you hear news of the other one dying in that town where everyone's into everyone else's business? And also, aren't you both standing in front of each other right now clearly alive and could we just get on with it, please, for the love of all that is holy and expedient?

What follows is a meeting that has been waiting seven years

to happen. They sit down on a "heap of moss" (how can that possibly be comfortable?) and begin with some small talk— *How about this weather we've been having? Seen any witches lately?* Finally, the conversation gets down to brass tacks—or as Hawthorne puts it "themes that were brooding deepest in their hearts"—when Dimmesdale asks Hester how she's been doing.

Hester *(pointing to her scarlet letter)*: How the hell do you *think* I've been doing, you dope? I've been wearing this stupid thing for seven goddamn years, and everyone who sees me shoots me looks of scorn powerful enough to knock my knickers off. How have you been?

Dimmesdale: Well, things have been waaay worse for me. At least that letter puts it out there for you. Me, I have to carry Adultery shame inside of me while all these adoring parishioners treat me like I'm the cute Beatle. Besides, everyone has practically forgotten what your letter stands for. Last week I overheard a couple of biddies talking about it. One of them insisted that it stood for Aerodynamic, the other one said, nope, it's Alley-Oop. Which doesn't even make sense!

Oh, if only I had a friend or even an enemy that I could talk to after spending day after day pretending to be Mr. Wonderful.

Hester: Well, now that you mention it, there is such a person and, well, he's your roommate.

Dimmesdale: What???

Hester: Oh, and one more thing, he was my husband.

Dimmesdale: *What??????????*

Beans thus spilt, Hester isn't sure if Dimmesdale is going to pitch them back at her or bake them into a delicious casserole (thus inventing Boston baked beans). Turns out, it's the former:

Dimmesdale: "Oh, Hester Prynne, thou little, little knowest

all the horror of this thing! And the shame!—the indelicacy!—the horrible ugliness of this exposure of a sick and guilty heart to the very eye that would gloat over it! Woman, woman, thou art accountable for this!—I cannot forgive thee!"

Hester *(begging)*: Oh Arthur, I—

The Classics Slacker *(to Hester)*: You know what? No. Hester, girlfriend, you are gonna have to sit this one out, because The Classics Slacker has a few choice words for ol' Dimmy.

The Classics Slacker *(to Dimmesdale)*: Listen, you mewling little baby man. You are not getting off the hook with the excuse of being a fictional character. Did you just seriously say that Hester doesn't know how hard this is for *you* and *you're* the one who has suffered the most and *you* aren't going to forgive *her* and are you freakin' kidding? If you have any shame left, you need to hang your head in it. Okay, The Classics Slacker's done here. Back to you two.

Hester implores Dimmesdale to forgive her, and he finally says he will (big whoop) and they sit together becoming kinda quietly anguished and at the same time a bit moony-eyed with each other and The Classics Slacker threw up a little in The Classics Slacker's mouth.

Problem is, Dimmy still has this situation of Chilly living under his roof and it's freaking him out. Twice he asks Hester to come up with a solution: "Think for me, Hester! Thou art strong. Resolve for me!" because she doesn't have enough on her plate, what with being an outcast single mom with a headstrong kiddo to look out for 24/7/365.

She tells him he can move to Europe. That's the ticket! It's a big world out there, she says. There's England (their native land) or Germany (tasty beer), France (ooh la la), "pleasant Italy." But Dimmy says, no way, I'm powerless, sinful, wretched, lost, flatulent. Plus, I have this job that "I dare not quit." He lists just every lame excuse.

It is beyond The Classics Slacker's comprehension why Hester doesn't just stand up and say, Okay, fine, I'm done. You wanna wallow, go ahead and wallow. Me, I'm choosing the company of these townspeople who loathe me and my loathsome erstwhile husband at this stage of the game. Don't say I didn't warn ya, because that's exactly what I just did. Adios, sucka.

But Hester doesn't do that or say that. Apparently—and Hawthorne confirms this—she's still in love with Dimmesdale. And so she launches into an even more impassioned pep talk. She tells him he could find a job as a preacher overseas. Or he can do something else altogether: "Write! Act!" *Sing! Direct!*

He is moved, finally. But there is yet another excuse holding him back. He doesn't want to go alone. She answers in a "deep whisper": "Thou shalt not go alone!"

It looks like behind even a very mediocre man there stands a great woman.

19
EVERYTHING'S COMING UP ROSES

In which Dimmy and Hester become lovebirds

With her sin advertised in a red capital letter across her chest, Hester walks around not really caring what anyone thinks about her because she's already ostracized. Dimmesdale, on the other hand, cares deeply about being judged for his sin—a sin that no one even knows about. Thus the difference between the two can be described thusly: Hester—strong; Dimmesdale—weenie.

Despite Dimmesdale's weak and whiny, meek and mewling constitution, Hester loves him, and in the chapter that Hawthorne calls "A Flood of Sunshine" everything's coming up roses for these two.

They are going to leave America, and the decision to blow that Puritan pop stand perks up Dimmesdale more than he's been perked since he visited Hester's garden of earthly delights seven years ago.

"Do I feel joy again? Methought the germ of it was dead in

me! Oh, Hester, thou art my better angel! I seem to have flung myself—sick, sin-stained, and sorrow-blackened—down upon these forest leaves, and to have risen up all made anew, and with new powers to glorify Him that hath been merciful! This is already the better life! Why did we not find it sooner?"

Dimmy, maybe just pull out a Shakespearean sonnet and read that, because your imagery is decidedly less than seductive. And the reason you two didn't find that "better life" sooner is because you're a worm who never admitted that Pearl is your daughter, remember?

You don't remember? Oh, how convenient.

Hester answers Dimmy that there's no point focusing on the past, saying it is best expressed in that song from the Disney musical *Frozen*—the one that The Classics Slacker's nieces sing all the time until it's stuck in The Classics Slacker's head for days.

Hester warbles, let it go, let it go, LET IT GOOOOOOOOO!

"Let us not look back, the past is gone! Wherefore should we linger upon it now? See! With this symbol I undo it all, and make it as if it had never been!"

Looking with joy to the future, she releases the clasp (A clasp! Who knew? The Classics Slacker thought it was stitched on) that holds that godawful scarlet letter and Frisbees it with such ferocity that it nearly lands in the brook. Next, she pulls off her cap and literally lets her hair down; the effect is lush. "Down it fell upon her shoulders, dark and rich, with at once a shadow and a light in its abundance, and imparting the charm of softness to her features."

Even the formerly judgmental sunshine wants to spend time with someone so babelicious. "All at once, as with a sudden smile of heaven, forth burst the sunshine, pouring a very flood into the obscure forest, gladdening each green leaf, transmuting the yellow fallen ones to gold, and gleaming adown the gray trunks of the solemn trees."

You know, The Classics Slacker really hates when sunshine is such a fair-weather friend because, jeez, the hypocrisy...

As Hester and Dimmesdale continue to declare words of love, birds suddenly appear, flowers bloom, frogs croak, chipmunks fornicate.

Ahh sweet romance!

And then, suddenly, Hester remembers Pearl. Honeymoon over.

You definitely want to get to know her, she says to Dimmesdale. She's your kid, after all.

Dimmesdale is reluctant, to say the least. He's almost backing away and shaking like the leaves that surround him. Kids and me, he says, not a good combo. "I have long shrunk from children, because they often show a distrust—a backwardness to be familiar with me. I have even been afraid of little Pearl!"

You'll be fine, Hester says. Pearl's a bit of a weirdo but you'll warm up to her. I pinky promise. "She will love thee dearly, and thou her. She is not far off. I will call her! Pearl! Pearl!"

Pearl had been playing in another part of the forest with various woodland creatures. One of them was a squirrel, which lobbed a nut onto her head. Ever the manuscript-padder, Hawthorne tosses in this rather irrelevant detail: "It was a last year's nut, and already gnawed by his sharp tooth."

When Pearl hears her mother's voice, she heads slowly toward her and...hey looky there, it's the clergyman! Papa don't preach! Who's my daddy?

As she draws nearer, step by step, Dimmy's terror grows. "I see the child," he says. "Yonder she is, standing in a streak of sunshine, a good way off *[and I wish she'd stay that way]* on the other side of the brook. So thou thinkest the child will love me?"

Reverend, take The Classics Slacker's advice. Bribery is a foolproof way to make kids like you. Just buy Pearl the *Frozen* DVD and you'll be all set.

20
KIDS DO THE DARNDEST THINGS

In which Pearl, though she be but little, is fierce

Our lovers have made a sweet plan for their future. Get out of Boston and hightail it over to Europe. Hester's hair is flowing, the scarlet letter is turning into compost, and whiny Reverend Arthur Dimmesdale is cheering up.

There's just one tiny detail to tend to at this point. The plot device that is the product of their union—Pearl.

Dimmy is shivering in his boots at the idea of meeting a seven-year-old girl, not as some minister, but as her father. Hester is doing a hard sell of Pearl's personality, probably for fear she's going to lose her man.

Pearl is strange, yes, but beautiful, no? See her wearing flowers from way off. So creative…Wow, it sure is taking her quite some time to come hither from over there yonder. What is taking her so long? PEARL!!! PEARL!!! YOU GET OVER HERE RIGHT NOW AND MEET YOUR FATHER!!!!!

It's all Dimmy can do not to turn and flee. You know, Hester, he says, as I mentioned, "children are not readily won to be familiar with me. They will not climb my knee, nor prattle in my ear, nor answer to my smile, but stand apart, and eye me strangely. Even little babes, when I take them in my arms, weep bitterly."

No surprise there. Kids do not like weenies, and Dimmesdale might as well be wearing a scarlet W. Long-suffering Hester continues to assure him, without a trace of exasperation, that everything is going to work out fine.

Okay, so then there's some more stuff about the brook and reflections in the brook and blah, blah the *brook*, and also, can we revisit whether or not Pearl is a real human child or an elf just one more time because we may not have belabored that issue enough yet.

Pearl is standing on the other side of the brook, and she's looking at her mom and she's looking at Dimmesdale and she is not having any of it. Because Pearl is not used to sharing her mama with anyone, let alone the mealy-mouthed minister WHO is taking away her mama's attention! And, also, Ma, WHERE'S your scarlet letter and WHAT have you done with your hair?

She doesn't say any of this, she just decides it's time for a big ol' honkin' temper tantrum!

Pearl "suddenly burst into a fit of passion, gesticulating violently, and throwing her small figure into the most extravagant contortions." (Hey kids, when having a tantrum, follow Pearl's example and make those contortions extra extravagant! Go big or go stand on the scaffold—it's the Puritan way!)

"She accompanied this wild outbreak with piercing shrieks, which the woods reverberated on all sides, so that, alone as she was in her childish and unreasonable wrath, it seemed as if a hidden multitude were lending her their sympathy and encouragement." So good to have Bambi and Thumper on your side.

At first Hester doesn't have a clue as to why Pearl is freaking out. Dimmesdale, Mr. Everything-Is-My-Fault-I'm-Full-of-Sin-and-Kids-Hate-Me, no doubt thinks he's the cause. But eventually Hester figures it out. Pearl had been pointing at the space where the scarlet letter used to be and notices that it's A for Absent. "Children will not abide any, the slightest, change in the accustomed aspect of things that are daily before their eyes. Pearl misses something which she has always seen me wear!"

Great, just do whatever it takes to make her stop screaming! Dimmy begs. "Pacify her, if thou lovest me!" So Hester "sadly" tells Pearl to pick up the scarlet letter from the ground and she reattaches it. Her diminishment is immediate. "As if there were a withering spell in the sad letter, her beauty, the warmth and richness of her womanhood, departed like fading sunshine, and a gray shadow seemed to fall across her."

She tells Dimmy she'll have to wear it just a little while longer until they are crossing the ocean, and then she'll pitch it into the Atlantic with a capital A. Like he cares when she throws it away; he just wants the kid to keep her trap shut.

Hester tucks her gorgeous hair back into her cap, too, in order to return to the mother Pearl knows.

Once Hester reverts to outcast-woman mode, Pearl calms down. She recognizes her mom as that sad woman with a symbol of eternal shame perpetually attached to her clothes and her hair tucked up in an unflattering Puritanical updo. Dimmesdale's fine too, because the kid isn't shrieking anymore, and who cares that Hester's miserable, right?

But whatever, at least she can bring Pearl and Daddy Dimmy together for a meaningful encounter. Except, well, it doesn't quite work out that way.

Wise beyond her years, Pearl first has a few pointed questions to ask. "Looking up with acute intelligence into her mother's face," she wants to know if the reverend will love them in front of the whole world, not just hidden in these woods.

"Will he go back with us, hand in hand, we three together, into the town?"

Gulp. Well, of course Hester tells her, sure, yes, he will, but, you know, just not right *now*, sweetie. And you can imagine how that goes over with this kid. Pearl refuses to move one inch toward Dimmesdale and so Hester goes into militia mode. "It was only by an exertion of force that her mother brought her up to him, hanging back, and manifesting her reluctance by odd grimaces."

Dimmesdale, "painfully embarrassed," tries to kiss Pearl on the forehead, "hoping that a kiss might prove a talisman to admit him into the child's kindlier regard." But she's like, Oh no you dih-int, and makes a big show of washing off his kiss in the brook.

Yes! You go, Pearl! You don't like something? You wash it away! Someone doesn't do right by you? You wash him away! You don't put up with their grownup excuses and hypocrisy and general gar-*bahj*, and that is one of a bazillion reasons The Classics Slacker is Team Pearl all the way!

21
LEAD ACTOR IN A MUSICAL

In which a lovestruck Dimmesdale gives an award-winning performance on the streets of the village

Dimmesdale leaves Hester and Pearl in the forest and heads back to town. He can't believe how lucky he is to be starting a new life with his new family. *Surely a flat in a European city will suit me more than a hut in this American wilderness*, he thinks. Hawthorne agrees. Dimmy's health is "so inadequate to sustain the hardships of a forest life." And everything about "his native gifts, his culture, and his entire development" were "more delicately adapted" to living in "civilization and refinement." In other words, Dimmesdale is no Daniel Boone.

Now, for the first time in, like, *forever*, he isn't beating himself up with shame, guilt, self-hatred, scourges, whips, chains, brooms, plungers, flyswatters, toothbrushes, etc. Dimmesdale notes that he has a new spring in his step and that he's seeing everything around him—the prison, the cemetery, the scaffold—

with new eyes, almost as though he just had laser surgery to correct nearsightedness.

He's like George Bailey on Christmas Eve. He's like Gene Kelly singing in the rain. He's as corny as Kansas in August, even though Kansas hasn't been discovered yet. He had often walked down these streets before, but the dirt always stayed beneath his feet before.

Dimmesdale feels like *People's* Sexiest Man of the Year, Seventeenth-Century Puritan New England edition, and he's acting the part, too. How?

• He's feisty: He bumps into a fellow deacon and has to hold himself back "from uttering certain blasphemous suggestions that rose into his mind, respecting the communion-supper." *And if we don't have triple chocolate lava cake for dessert, Padre, you can stick that chalice where the sun don't shine!*

• He's flighty: He encounters one of his elderly parishioners who is looking for some impromptu churching. But he can "recall no text of Scripture, nor aught else, except a brief, pithy, and, as it then appeared to him, unanswerable argument against the immortality of the human soul." *Lady, that stuff I kept yapping about how life goes on after death and how we'll all meet again in heaven? It's a load of crap!*

• He's horny: He spots a virgin from his flock. "She was fair and pure as a lily that had bloomed in Paradise." The Classics Slacker bets she was. Dimmesdale feels a powerful urge to "drop into her tender bosom a germ of evil that would be sure to blossom darkly soon, and bear black fruit betimes." Hello? Dimmy? Remember the promises you just made with your new girlfriend, Hester? Don't be a dick already. And leave the gardening to the professionals.

• He's jolly: He wants to knock back a beer or two and swear with a sailor he sees. "Mr. Dimmesdale longed, at least, to shake hands with the tarry blackguard, and recreate himself with a few improper jests, such as dissolute sailors so abound with, and a volley of good, round, solid, satisfactory, and heaven-defying oaths!" Why, that *would* be fun!

Dimmesdale doesn't actually give in to any of these crazy urges, but still, it's a good thing the ship bound for England is going to whisk him out of there in four days. The timing of the trip is perfect for another reason, too, although Dimmesdale won't tell us why. But Hawthorne does, because he's just that kind of author, and The Classics Slacker, for one, loves that about him:

"It was because, on the third day from the present, he was to preach the Election Sermon [to vote is divine?]; and, as such an occasion formed an honorable epoch in the life of a New England Clergyman, he could not have chanced upon a more suitable mode and time of terminating his professional career."

Fine, go out with a bang, The Classics Slacker always says.

But before he can get home to pack and write, he has one more wackadoodle meetup, and that is with witchy Mistress Hibbins, who seems to know everything that's goin' on everywhere with everyone. She tells him that the next time he's planning to go to the forest he should invite her along. "Without taking overmuch upon myself my good word will go far towards gaining any strange gentleman a fair reception from yonder potentate you wot of."

Say wot?

Wotever. While Dimmesdale admits that he was in the forest, he denies that he had gone there to pal around with the Black Man or his bevy of witches. Now if you'll excuse me, Mistress Hibbins, I'm heading to the sanctuary of my home, where there is of course no sanctuary because that creepy and malignant

Chillingworth still lives there.

When he arrives, the Leech gives the minister a surprisingly warm welcome. Wow, he says, lookin' a bit under the weather there, my friend. How's about I make you a nice little tonic? And Dimmesdale is all, like, Nuh uh, thanks, I'm good.

They have a lovely little chat about the importance of the upcoming "Election discourse." But they both know what they're talking about without actually saying, *She told you, right?* and *Right, she told me.* This exchange represents Hawthorne's brief master class on subtext.

Chillingworth finally leaves Dimmesdale in relative peace, at which point the reverend orders a huge dinner to be delivered and proceeds to eat *con* newfound *gusto.* Then he tears up his old Election Sermon and starts to write a brand new one, because when inspiration strikes, ya gotta grab it, beauty sleep (among other things) be damned.

22
I'M WEARING ARMANI

*In which Election Day gives everyone a chance to
show off their duds*

Yay! Election Day is here! But we don't see voters waiting in
line to slip ballots into boxes or watching the returns come
in on TV. The main event of the "holiday" is just a sad-sack procession. "The Governor and the magistrates are to go by," Hester
tells Pearl in a pathetic effort to gin up her excitement, "and the
ministers, and all the great people and the good people [and the
just-okay people], with the music and the soldiers marching
before them." Zzzzz. The Macy's Thanksgiving Day Parade this
ain't, but the Election Day procession serves as a bright spot in
the dreary existence of Hester and her neighbors.

The rest of the chapter is basically a summary of "What
Everyone Wore." The "general tint" of the Puritan townsfolk, aka
the "human life in the market-place," was the "sad gray, brown,
or black of the English emigrants," even though they are alleged-

ly celebrating a holiday. Appearing in much more festive garb are the Native Americans. "A party of Indians—in their savage finery of curiously embroidered deer-skin robes, wampum belts, red and yellow ochre, and feathers—stood apart." That's for sure. Puritans, except for Hester, could never employ color successfully. Not to mention accessorize.

Hester was "clad in a garment of coarse gray cloth," which does nothing for her. "Not more by its hue than by some indescribable peculiarity in its fashion, it had the effect of making her fade personally out of sight and outline." Needless to say, her scarlet letter is clasped on tight in its customary position. And although it provides the color lacking in the clothing of her fellow citizens, Hester is so over it. The A, which has long been Attached is soon to be Adios.

Indeed, Hester has some choice thoughts for the townspeople: "Look your last on the scarlet letter and its wearer! Yet a little while, and she will be beyond your reach! A few hours longer and the deep, mysterious ocean will quench and hide for ever the symbol which ye have caused to burn on her bosom!"

In case you are in need of translation, dear Puritan townsfolk, please allow The Classics Slacker to be of service. What Hester would love to be saying to you is, in effect, So long, suckas! Eat my dust!

Waiting around for the parade to start, Pearl, who is "decked out with airy gaety" has some thoughts of her own. The reader can almost hear the kid's inner monologue at this point: *Parade? Check. With ministers? Check. This is the perfect occasion for Reverend Now-I-See-You, Now-I-Don't to acknowledge me publicly the way he has acknowledged me privately.*

To Hester's endless irritation, Pearl starts badgering her again. *Is he going to greet us, Mother?* "Will he hold out both his hands to me, as when thou ledst me to him from the brook-side?"

Mom, of course, is all, like, Nuh *uh*, kid. Even though the author of this book says that your dress "seems an effluence, or inevitable development and outward manifestation of your character, no more to be separated from you than the many-hued brilliancy from a butterfly's wing, or the painted glory from the leaf of a bright flower," Dimmesdale won't talk to you. Got it? And you better not talk to him, either.

Pearl's like, Hmm, okay, so, let me get this straight…he holds our hands in pitch black darkness on the scaffold, he talks to us and even kisses me in the woods where only squirrels can see us. But then in daylight among people he ignores us? What's up with that?

Hester tells her, Zip it, kid! "Thou understandest not these things." Oh, The Classics Slacker thinks she does. She understandest thosem things very well.

Pearl then offers a perfectly succinct characterization of Dimmesdale, demonstrating that she's on track to be a top-notch screenwriter someday: "A strange, sad man is he, with his hand always over his heart!"

Yup, Pearl, kiddo, you got that right. Your dad's a piece of work. Period. End of discussion.

But Hester is about to have an even more worrisome conversation than any she's had with Pearl. It starts with the appearance of her ever-so-creepy secret bygone husband.

"Roger Chillingworth [nooooo!], the physician [yes, we know, also goes by "the Leech"], was seen to enter the market-place in close and familiar talk with the commander of the questionable vessel."

Ohhh, no. What is happening here? What is the questionable vessel in question? Turns out it's the very same one that Hester and Pearl and Dimmesdale plan to take en route to their happily-ever-after life in Europe.

Chillingworth wanders off and the commander—who "wore a profusion of ribbons on his garment, and gold lace on his hat, which was also encircled by a gold chain, and surmounted with a feather" (The Classics Slacker stands corrected; some Puritans *can* accessorize)—approaches Hester and gives her the good news: "I must bid the steward make ready one more berth than you bargained for! No fear of scurvy or ship fever this voyage. What with the ship's surgeon and this other doctor [meaning Chillingworth]..."

Ohh, *great* news, Captain Fancy Hat, and there's Chillingworth sporting a Cheshire cat grin: "...she beheld old Roger Chillingworth himself, standing in the remotest corner of the market-place and smiling on her; a smile which—across the wide and bustling square, and through all the talk and laughter, and various thoughts, moods, and interests of the crowd—conveyed secret and fearful meaning."

And Hester is no doubt thinking, Oh, HELL no! I am NOT okay with my uneven-shouldered ex joining the party on our love cruise to happiness.

But what's an oppressed and A-shamed Puritan gal to do? The tickets are nonrefundable and Hester didn't even think of buying travel insurance.

23
WALK ON BY

In which Hester is definitely not feeling the holiday

The parade is beginning! Where's the guy selling cotton candy? Hester is flipped out to learn that an unwelcome guest is joining her escape party. But before she can give it too much thought, she hears badly played military music in the distance. How bad is it? "It comprised a variety of instruments, perhaps imperfectly adapted to one another, and played with no great skill."

Still, Hawthorne tells us, the music serves its purpose: "…that of imparting a higher and more heroic air to the scene…" More importantly for Hester, the collective banging and clanging of the parade presages the arrival of one very special minister—her own Dimmesdale walking toward her, as if they are symbolically beginning their new life together.

But first she has to wait for a phalanx of soldiers to march past, followed by the magistrates of the town. "These primitive statesmen…who were elevated to power by the early choice of the people, seem to have been not often brilliant, but distinguished by a ponderous sobriety, rather than activity of intellect." No, these states*men*—and you know they're all *men*—are not smart, but they certainly are dour, and that's just how these townsfolk like their local officials.

Finally, bringing up the rear, Reverend Dimmesdale himself! There he is! She sees him! And you know what else? He is lookin' *good* today!

"Never had Mr. Dimmesdale exhibited such energy as was seen in the gait and air with which he kept his pace in the procession. There was no feebleness of step as at other times; his frame was not bent, nor did his hand rest ominously upon his heart." Hubba-hubba.

Hester's heart is all aflutter as her dear Dimmy comes closer and closer and...he passes her. Not a smile, not a glance, not the slightest acknowledgment of Hester's existence as he fairly prances on by. Is he just not into her anymore? "She thought of the dim forest, with its little dell of solitude, and love, and anguish, and the mossy tree-trunk, where, sitting hand-in-hand, they had mingled their sad and passionate talk with the melancholy murmur of the brook...She hardly knew him now!"

And isn't that just like a man? He's all lovey-dovey whilst sharing a mossy log in the dim forest, but then becomes all *Hester-who-now?* in public. Pearl, who is growing up to be quite the budding feminist, sees what her mother sees and she's all, like, Seriously, Ma, what is *his* problem? And Hester shushes her little Gloria Steinem with the old "what happens in the forest stays in the forest" B.S., a terrible yet all-too-common message used by parents throughout the ages to quiet their kids in public places.

Anyway, it's time for the big Election Sermon! Hurry and pull up a pew! This oughta be good! Good except for the fact that Dimmy doesn't even save a seat for Hester. Another slap in the face. "The sacred edifice was too much thronged to admit another auditor" so she had to take up "a position close beside the scaffold of the pillory." *Crap, here I am again.*

Hawthorne spares the reader the actual words of Dimmy's pious gabfest, but he doesn't spare us Hester's gooey reaction to it:

"Muffled as the sound was by its passage through the church walls, Hester Prynne listened with such intenseness, and sympathized so intimately, that the sermon had throughout a meaning for her, entirely apart from its indistinguishable words." Ugh.

By the way, Pearl is having a swell time on the Election Day holiday. She's clapping her hands; she's dancing to the bad music; she's rising like "a floating sea-bird": "Whenever Pearl saw anything to excite her ever active and wandering curiosity, she flew thitherward."

Seeing her, the Puritans try hard not to smile. But even if they break, they still pronounce her "a demon offspring." Kid, you're adorable 'n' all, but we're Puritans 'n' all, so we still have to assume you're aligned with Satan, 'kay? No offense.

Hawthorne refers to Pearl flying several more times in this chapter, and it's a good thing, too. Because the shipmaster—yes, the very one in charge of the ship that the Dimmesdale family will be taking to England—is so taken with Pearl that he "attempted to lay hands on her, with purpose to snatch a kiss." Ew. That is so not cool.

Fortunately, Pearl is too fast for him. He found it "as impossible to touch her as to catch a humming-bird in the air." She both eludes him and charms him into giving away his gold chain in exchange for bringing a message to her mother. He says, "I spake again with the black-a-visaged, hump-shouldered doctor," using questionable past-tense verbiage and more than the legal allotment of hyphens in a sentence. Turns out, Chillingworth is going to pay for Dimmesdale's passage. "So let thy mother take no thought, save for herself and thee."

Rather than receive this news as "Score! More money to spend at the ship's bar," Hester is upset for the second time. Election Day has been a super sucky holiday. Dimmy is ignoring her, Chilly is crashing her love boat, and then there's this fresh hell: Out-of-towners closing in on her to gape at her confounded letter A. "After exhausting other modes of amusement, [they] now thronged about Hester Prynne with rude and boorish intrusiveness." *Okay, everybody, we've watched the parade and rode the Ferris wheel, what's next? Should we go stare at that lady with the A on her chest?*

Sailors, from whom you would expect better behavior, "came and thrust their sunburnt and desperado-looking faces" at her. Then the white bro culture influenced the Native Americans in the crowd to take up the same bad behavior; they "fastened their snake-like black eyes on Hester's bosom."

Great. Although it sucks to have guys checking out your boobs, at least the Native Americans didn't know that the A was a mark of shame. Quite the opposite. They thought "perhaps, that the wearer of this brilliantly embroidered badge must needs be a personage of high dignity among her people." Like an Astronaut.

And where is Dimmesdale while his girlfriend is enduring this super awkward situation? Only up on his pulpit yet again enjoying the adoration of the crowd.

A is for Aaarrggghhh!

24
SHOW AND TELL

In which Dimmesdale takes it off, takes it all off

Reverend Dimmesdale finishes up his Election Sermon and everyone is buzzing. They can't stop talking about how this was the world's greatest sermon ever given ever. The congregants even light matches and hold them above their heads and wave them side to side in unison in an undulating tide of glory, just like at a really cool rock concert.

Yeah, no, that's not what happened at all. But it was an extremely popular speech.

Problem is, it seems to have taken quite a lot out of Dimmy, who, as we have seen, has never been the hearty sort. "The inspiration which had held him up, until he should have delivered the sacred message…was withdrawn, now that it had so faithfully performed its office." The result: "[He] was hardly a man with life in him, that tottered on his path so nervelessly."

What gives? He marched into the church all bouncy and

proud, and he exits the church as if his femurs have been removed. It's all a big mystery and with Hawthorne at the pen who can really tell. But it's obvious that Dimmy, for whatever reason, isn't going on any six-week boat trip to England any time soon. The procession begins to make its way toward the town hall for a "solemn banquet" (probably with a cash bar, which definitely sucks). There is a great outburst of approbation for Reverend Dimmesdale from the crowd.

"Never, from the soil of New England had gone up such a shout! Never, on New England soil had stood the man so honored by his mortal brethren as the preacher!" Time to raise your lighters again, you wacky Puritans, and start a-wavin' them! *Freebird!!!*

Okay, so, The Classics Slacker hopes you're sitting down, because some major stuff is about to happen…

The fussy town leaders Bellingham and Reverend Wilson both try to help Dimmesdale because it really looks as if he's about to pass out. But he refuses their help and instead stumbles toward ye olde scaffold. There he calls out for Hester and Pearl to join him.

Hester rushes to be with Dimmesdale, and Pearl lets go of any lingering irritation with her papa's hesitancy to acknowledge her in the past: "The child, with the bird-like motion, which was one of her characteristics [yes, we know], flew to him, and clasped her arms about his knees."

It's a lovely and very touching moment, so of course Chillingworth has to show up to ruin the whole damn thing.

"Wave back that woman!" he commands Dimmesdale. "Cast off this child! All shall be well! Do not blacken your fame, and perish in dishonor! I can yet save you! Would you bring infamy on your sacred profession?"

Does our pale pastor heed his doctor's orders? He does not. Weak though he appears, Dimmesdale *finally* stands up to

Chillingworth, basically telling him, Yeah, Doc? May I call you the Leech? How about you piss *all* the way off, huh?

Good on you, Reverend Dimmesdale. If The Classics Slacker is being honest, The Classics Slacker didn't think you had it in you.

Unfortunately, by resisting Chilly, he may have used up the last iota of his strength. He pulls Hester in close as he whispers to her what sound very much like his last words: "Is not this better than what we dreamed of in the forest?"

And Hester cannot BELIEVE what she is hearing. She's all, like, *Better? How is this better? You dying on this &^*%$#@ scaffold is better than us moving to England? What are you, nuts? We were going to take high tea at Fortnum and Mason. Shop at Harrods. Punt on the Thames. Drink beer at The Bull and Testicle. No, dying on this godforsaken scaffold isn't better, you dimwit!!!*

Instead of a love cruise back to Jolly Olde England, our gal Hester is going home with a consolation prize, courtesy of her dear, about-to-be-departed Dimmesdale. Tell her what she's won, Dimmy:

"People of New England! Ye, that have loved me!—ye, that have deemed me holy!—behold me here, the one sinner of the world! At last!—at last!—I stand upon the spot where, seven years since, I should have stood; here, with this woman, whose arm, more than the little strength wherewith I have crept hitherward, sustains me, at this dreadful moment, from grovelling down upon my face!"

It's a dreadful moment indeed, but it's better than breaking out the scourge again. Dimmesdale goes on to say that everyone who reviled Hester because of her scarlet letter should take a look at this! He tears open his coat to reveal a scarlet letter of his very own!

There's a collective horrified gasp* and with that, Dimmy, in the arms of Hester and Pearl, goes off to meet his maker, you know, the one he's heard so much about.

   * The Classics Slacker must pause here for just a moment to ask: Didst no one see-eth that coming? What with the whole hand-on-the-heart business being mentioned over and over and over?

25

CONCLUSION:

WHERE ARE THEY NOW?

In which Hawthorne takes your questions
about what happened to his characters

Dimmy is dead. He is surrounded by his would-be wife and his child. He has delivered the greatest sermon ever. He has reached the pinnacle of both his personal and professional life. They are up on a stage in front of a captive audience. A perfect scene for dropping the final curtain. The end.

Except who should come out from behind the curtain but Hawthorne himself. He of the 15,000-word explanatory introduction feels the need to offer up some more words (thankfully not nearly as many) to clear up any lingering questions for any inquiring readers. Such a considerate guy.

Inquiring reader: *What was the deal with the letter A on Dimmesdale's chest? How did it get there? Was it the work of a sa-*

distic *Acupuncturist? Or did Dimmesdale inflict it on himself, in a colonial precursor to cutting? Did Chillingworth possibly render it "through the agency of magic and poisonous drugs"?*

Hawthorne: "The reader may choose among these theories." (The Classics Slacker chooses to believe that Dimmesdale drew it on himself with a red Sharpie.)

Inquiring reader: *What happened to Chillingworth after Dimmesdale died, leaving him out of the revenge business?*

Hawthorne: "All his strength and energy—all his vital and intellectual force—seemed at once to desert him, insomuch that he positively withered up, shrivelled away and almost vanished from mortal sight, like an uprooted weed that lies wilting in the sun." (Mean kids take note.)

Inquiring reader: *What happened to the demon elf-child Pearl? Did she become an apprentice to witchy Mistress Hibbins and take up flying on a broomstick?*

Hawthorne: "Pearl was [living on the continent] married, and happy, and mindful of her mother; and she would most joyfully have entertained that sad and lonely mother at her fireside."

Inquiring reader: *Then why didn't Pearl joyfully entertain her sad and lonely mother at her fireside?*

Hawthorne: "Hester Prynne had returned [without Pearl] and taken up her long-forsaken shame."

Inquiring reader: *What??*

Hawthorne: "There was a more real life for Hester Prynne, here, in New England than where Pearl had found a home. Here had been her sin; here, her sorrow; and here was yet to be her penitence."

Inquiring reader: *You've got to be kidding me.*
Hawthorne: "I kiddeth thee not."

Inquiring reader: *Okay. But at least tell me that she didn't continue to wear that scarlet letter* **A** *Ad nauseum?*
Hawthorne: "Never afterwards did it quit her bosom."

Inquiring reader: *What!? Why?*
Hawthorne: "In the lapse of the toilsome, thoughtful, and self-devoted years that made up Hester's life, the scarlet letter ceased to be a stigma which attracted the world's scorn and bitterness, and became a type of something to be sorrowed over, and looked upon with awe, yet with reverence too."

Inquiring reader: *Okay, well, if you say so. No husband, no kid, what did she do all day?*
Hawthorne: "As Hester Prynne had no selfish ends, not lived in any measure for her own profit and enjoyment, people brought all their sorrows and perplexities, and besought her counsel, as one who had herself gone through a mighty trouble."

Inquiring reader: *So Hester became the town psychologist?*
Hawthorne: "Exactly."

Inquiring reader: *The tombstone under which Hester and Dimmesdale are buried together has an inscription: "On a field, sable, the letter A, gules." What does that mean?*
Hawthorne: "I have no idea."

THE OBLIGATORY AUTHOR BIOGRAPHY

Open any classic book and you will discover a timeline of the author's life. Do not read it. These biographies all sound the same and they all go something like this:

The Life of Nathaniel Hawthorne
July 4, 1804: Nathaniel Hathorne (not a typo) is born in Salem, Massachusetts. He is the second child of U.S. Navy captain Nathaniel Hathorne and Elizabeth Manning Hathorne, who show unfair favoritism by gifting Nate with an additional consonant and a used car for his sixteenth birthday.

1820: Hawthorne writes and publishes *The Spectator*, a newsmagazine that he distributes to friends and family. With a circulation of eighteen and no advertising revenue to speak of, it runs for one month before Hawthorne closes it down, muttering "Well, that was a lousy idea..."

1821: Hawthorne enrolls at Bowdoin College. His friends and fellow students there include future U.S. President Franklin Pierce and poet Henry Wadsworth Longfellow. Proving yet again, it's never who you know.

1825: Hawthorne graduates from Bowdoin and moves back in with family in Salem. He spends the next ten years in isolation, rarely seeing friends or relatives, on account of their less-than-enthusiastic reaction to his magazine and ongoing disputes about lapsed subscriptions.

1828: Hawthorne publishes two short stories as Nathaniel Hathorne. From then on, he uses the name "Hawthorne" personally and professionally. Speculation as to the reason for this change ranges from Nate just liking the way "w" sounded to a theory that the letter had incriminating evidence about Hathorne that it threatened to make public.

1839: Hawthorne takes a job at the Boston Custom-House. He later states that he misheard and thought it was a trendy restaurant, the Boston Custard-House.

1842: After a three-year engagement, Hawthorne marries Sophia Peabody, a painter. He tries to convince Sophia to change her name to Sowphia as a wedding gift to him, but she tells him she already bought him cufflinks engraved with her first name.

1844: Sophia gives birth to the couple's first child, a daughter named Una. Sophia warns the new dad, "Nate, don't even start with spelling it 'Unaw,' okay?"

1846: The couple's second child is born. He is nameless for the first few months of his life until his parents agree on "Julian." Hawthorne wanted to name him "Buster," but he lost two out of three in rock-paper-scissors. Sophia puts the kibosh on spelling it "Juwlian."

1846: Hawthorne takes a position at the Salem Custom-House. On his first day at work, he groans, "This isn't a restaurant? Oh man, I can't believe I screwed up twice..."

1849: Hawthorne is dismissed from the Salem Custom-House in a political shakeup, and also because he kept asking clients, "Saved room for dessert?"

1849: Hawthorne's mother dies and he falls into a deep depression. He begins writing *The Scarlet Letter,* despite his wife cautioning him that it "might not be the best story to wallow in while fighting off pervasive gloom, sweetheart."

1850: *The Scarlet Letter* is published and is an instant bestseller, a media phenomenon that will not be replicated until the release of *Fifty Shades of Grey.*

1851: Herman Melville, whose love of Hawthorne borders on obsession, publishes *Moby Dick.* He dedicates the book to Hawthorne, "With gratitude to NH, from the whale 'n' me."

1853: Franklin Pierce takes office as president and awards his college friend an appointment as U.S. Consul in Liverpool. The

Hawthorne family sails to England, where they are disappointed to reach the legendary port city more than a century before the Beatles arrive on the scene.

1857: Hawthorne loses his position after Pierce loses the Democratic nomination for reelection; Hawthorne bitterly complains that he doesn't see "what one thing has to do with the other."

1860: Hawthorne's novel *The Marble Faun* is published. He is immediately sued by the letter "w" for not spelling it "Fawn." Hawthorne represents himself at trial and wins the case in a courtroom confrontation with his accuser, declaring, "A *faun* is a figure in Roman mythology and a *fawn* is a baby deer…they're two different things!"

May 19, 1864: Nathaniel Hawthorne dies in Plymouth, New Hampshire, while vacationing with Franklin Pierce. His last words were reported to be, "Frankie, if you don't shut up about losing the nomination, I swear, my head's gonna explode…"

ALSO BY THE CLASSICS SLACKER:

The Classics Slacker Reads Madame Bovary
The Classics Slacker Reads Moby Dick

Upcoming books in *The Classics Slacker* series:

The Classics Slacker Reads Anna Karenina
The Classics Slacker Reads The Count of Monte Cristo
The Classics Slacker Reads The Great Gatsby
The Classics Slacker Reads The Picture of Dorian Gray
The Classics Slacker Reads Silas Marner
The Classics Slacker Reads A Tale of Two Cities
The Classics Slacker Reads Ulysses
The Classics Slacker Reads War and Peace
The Classics Slacker Reads Wuthering Heights

Made in the USA
Middletown, DE
14 March 2022